# FROM FEAR
# TO FAITH

## JUERGEN SIMONSON

### Foreword by
### Lord Coggan

The Canterbury Press
Norwich

© Juergen Simonson 1995

First published 1995 by The Canterbury Press Norwich
(a publishing imprint of Hymns Ancient & Modern Limited,
a registered charity)
St Mary's Works, St Mary's Plain,
Norwich, Norfolk, NR3 3BH

Juergen Simonson has asserted his right under the
Copyright Designs and Patents Act, 1988, to be identified
as Author of this Work

British Library Cataloguing in Publication Data

A catalogue record for this book is available
from the British Library

ISBN 1–85311–103–1


Typeset by Datix International Limited
Bungay, Suffolk and
Printed in Great Britain by
St Edmundsbury Press Ltd, Bury St Edmunds, Suffolk

For my grandchildren
and
in memory of Henry Ball
(died 2.9.92)

# FOREWORD

*by the Right Reverend Lord Coggan,*
*former Archbishop of Canterbury*

ONE of my most moving memories of the immediately post-war years can be described briefly: The scene was the Chapel of a theological college. The service was the Eucharist. Side by side at the communion rail knelt two young men. Only a short while before, one had been a Nazi youth leader in Germany; now he was an ordinand struggling with all the problems which must beset anyone whose transition from one world to another had been so dramatic. The other was also a German, but of Jewish extraction studying, like the man next to him, for ordination in the Church of England. Both, reconciled to God and reconciled to one another, held out their empty hands to receive the tokens of God's grace and to feed on Christ by faith with thanksgiving. These two men lived together, studied together, worshipped together in the college – united in Christ. The second of these two men is the writer of this book.

You will not be surprised that I have read the typescript of *From Fear to Faith* with the deepest interest and that I count it a privilege to write its 'Foreword'. The friendship which Juergen Simonson extended to a young German who, not long before, would have hounded him to death illustrates the power of forgiveness and the strength of unity within the Body of Christ. To read the first part of this book is to be reminded of the horrors of World War Two – and they should never be forgotten. But it is also to watch the strong patience of the Hound of Heaven in laying hold and keeping hold on the young man Juergen who was to be his devoted follower in the ensuing years. If you are like me, you will find it hard to put down the first section of this book.

But if you were to put down the book at the point where Part One ends, you would miss a great deal. Part Two, though less dramatic than Part One, is full of interest. I will tell you why.

The reason is that Juergen Simonson has touched life at points which are of great human interest and, I would venture to say, of critical importance for the future not only of the Church but of society as a whole. I mention three of them:

(a) *Theological education.* Juergen obtained the London B.D. degree, as well as the Associateship of his college, in 1952 – no mean achievement when it is remembered that he had to study and write his examination papers in a language other than his native tongue. Some of the best years of his life were given to work in Melville Hall, Ibadan, a key institution in the training of Nigeria's future clergy, and further years, under very different conditions, in the training at Chislehurst of tomorrow's missionaries. Such theological institutions hold the key to the health of the Church they serve.

(b) *Service abroad.* Juergen and Jean Simonson have always had a clear vision of 'one world, one Church'. They know that to invest a spell of years in the service of one of the younger churches is not only to give of one's best to that church but to enrich oneself and one's ministry beyond all telling. The investment is often a costly one, but its dividends are high.

(c) *Parish work.* In addition to the years of his curacy, Juergen and Jean spent twenty-one years in two big South London parishes in the diocese of Southwark. Such work is at the very heart of the Church's mission. The clergy are very often at the receiving end of music-hall jokes, and if they have a sense of humour they can join in the laughter. But more often and more seriously, their calling is misunderstood, misrepresented, lampooned. In truth, parochial ministry is the chief glory of the Church. Day by day, week in week out, the Vicar is at his job of prayer, of ministry of Word and Sacrament, of comfort and consolation, sharing the joys and sorrows of his people in an intimacy given to no others. That was precisely what occupied the writer of this book for more than two decades – and he gloried in it.

I welcome *From Fear to Faith* very warmly. It is the story of a man with a lively mind, with a happy marriage and family, a man who has come through deep waters, who has loved his ministry and still does. It is a book which deals with life's realities and invites us to join its writer in one of his favourite quotes from Dag Hammerskjöld:

'For all that has been – thanks!
To all that will be – yes!'

# CONTENTS

# PREFACE

GRANDPA, when can I see your book?' Ben, my little grandson, keeps pestering me with this question. Yes, in the first place I have written these reminiscences for my family just as my father did for his grandchildren ('The Last Judgment' by Werner Simonson, 1969). Our background is somewhat out of the ordinary – German, victims of the Nazis, migration to England, a new homeland. These experiences are part of their background, too. It is important that they are not just a faint myth for them, but that they know about them and that they accept them as part of their family history. But apart from the family a number of friends who know a little bit about my past have graciously encouraged me to write it up and make it available to a wider audience. This, however, is a purely private and personal reason for writing this book and, one could argue, not a good enough reason for publishing it.

A far more important reason is to make a contribution to the historical record of a very strange period in the events of this century. It is nearly 50 years since Hitler perished in the Chancellery in Berlin and the dreadful Nazi regime came to an end. Since then a new generation has grown up who have no personal knowledge and first hand experience of that evil power that plunged the whole world into untold suffering and total war. Hitler's name is still common knowledge, but more through hearsay than through any direct involvement in the events of that period. Looking back on it now it seems extraordinary that the Nazi regime lasted for only 12 years which in the course of history is nothing. And so one could be easily tempted to consign those years to the past. And yet, for those who lived in Nazi Germany at that time it seemed endless. In fact, there were moments when one wondered whether it was ever going to end.

Many books have been written about the dictatorship of Hitler. Martyrs have been commemorated, victims and refugees have recorded their personal memories. I am adding one further piece to it because I believe that it is so important for this and future generations never to forget the scourge which one dictator could inflict on millions of people. The Arch-

bishop of Canterbury at a recent commemoration of Dietrich
Bonhoeffer and Bishop George Bell said 'The majority of
Christians and others caved in under the regime of evil, violence
and terror which sent millions to the gas chambers and which
for ever will shame the history of Western Europe. Fifty years
on I wonder if we can claim that the lessons have been
learned.' It is, therefore, necessary that even after 50 years
further voices are being heard to remind us of this 'shame' and
through these personal stories to convey what it was like to
live under a totalitarian regime.

The former Allies have recently celebrated the 50th anniversary of the D-Day landings. In my diary I write on 6th June
1944 'The great day has come.' The day that we had been
waiting for over twelve long years, the day that spelt hope and
perhaps freedom. It was not yet the end of Hitler nor of the
war. More suffering and terror lay ahead, but somehow I
knew on that day that it was bound to be a turning point and
that, God willing, it would lead eventually to liberty and a
new life. For me it meant not only physical liberation months
later, but a gradual spiritual transformation. And that is why
this book is above all the record of one Christian's pilgrimage
from captivity to freedom, from darkness to light, from fear to
faith. It is the story of God's dealings with one young man
whose life seemed in jeopardy. But God stepped in and out of
this rescue, both bodily and spiritual, has come an incredibly
rich and rewarding life. I am anxious to share this with my
readers and give God the glory.

Lastly, I hope that this book will also be a kaleidoscope of
contemporary Church history. We are sometimes rather dismiss-
ive about the state of the Church in our time. I want to remind
us of the enormous changes that have taken place in the
Church during the second half of this century. It is not all a
dull and dismal picture. There is much that is positive and
encouraging. I am glad that I was called to serve God in his
Church during the last 40 years and I hope that my personal
impressions of the Church at home and abroad will testify to
the fact that God is at work in our time and that he constantly
has more grace to offer.

*October 1994*                                              J.W.D.S.

# PART ONE

# I

# Childhood in Forst

BORN in 1924 I grew up during that volatile period between the end of the First World War and the Versailles Treaty and the worsening of the political and economic situation in Germany leading to the rise of Hitler and the Nazi regime. I remember vaguely several German Elections, the proliferation of political parties and the alarming increase in unemployment. I had a great admiration for von Hindenburg, the Field Marshall of the First World War and venerable German President who seemed to me like a rock in that rather unstable situation. My parents were probably aware of the growing influence of the NSDAP (Nationalist Socialist German Labour Party) and their steadily increasing share of votes in the elections (from 2% in 1928 to 33% in 1932!). But I was too young to appreciate what went on in politics. All the more as we were living in a small town in East Germany where one was somewhat removed from the centre of affairs. But that blissful ignorance was soon to change.

Both my parents came from good and comfortable homes. My grandfathers were both in the legal profession. Grandfather Simonson was a Senior Judge at the German Supreme Court in Leipzig. Grandfather Schweling was a Senior Judge at the County Court in Naumburg, not far from Leipzig. Much further back my mother descended from the famous organist and composer Jan Pieter Sweelinck. One of her more immediate forebears was Ludwig Windthorst who in the last century was regarded as one of the outstanding German paliamentarians. Quite recently, on the anniversary of his death (1891) a commemoration took place which was attended by a number of German politicians and several Catholic Bishops (he was also a leading Catholic layman). My mother was Catholic, my father Protestant. I was totally unaware that he came from a Jewish background. My grandparents had converted to the Christian religion when they were young. But that issue did not figure in our minds until the Nazis appeared on the scene.

The much greater problem at that time seemed to be for a Protestant to marry a Catholic. I was told that when they got married my father refused to sign on the dotted line that the children of this marriage would be brought up in the Catholic faith. What I do remember clearly was an occasion in my grandparents' home in Naumburg when my mother was seriously ill with pneumonia and was nursed by Catholic nuns. They told her very firmly that this illness was God's punishment for marrying a Protestant! Fortunately we have made some progress in ecumenical relations since those days.

We visited my respective grandparents quite often. I recall blissful summer holidays in Naumburg which was a delightful provincial town in Thuringia with a famous Cathedral. My grandparents came from Westphalia (they later retired to Muenster) and my grandfather spoke with a typical Westphalian accent. He played the Ocarina, an instrument which one does not see very much nowadays. He seemed a venerable old gentleman although he was probably only in his sixties. My grandmother was a warm-hearted, somewhat eccentric lady. But I thought she was the ideal grandmother. I can still see her sitting at the piano and playing Grieg. One year there was a big summer festival in Naumburg. At the opening parade I proudly marched with her at the head of the procession. She had no inhibitions. I loved the house and the garden and spent many sunny summer days in their lovely garden. We used to go for outings into the beautiful surrounding countryside. One favourite place to visit was the Rudelsburg, an old castle. I spotted it recently from the train on my way to Leipzig and it brought many memories of those carefree days.

My other grandparents lived in a very large apartment in Leipzig. It had long corridors with large rooms leading off – a dining room, my grandmother's sitting room, a very large salon, my grandfather's study lined with books. Then several bedrooms leading to another semi-detached flat where my aunt Ilse lived. She travelled, especially to Italy. She wrote about her travels and she was a sculptor. She had her own workroom as part of the flat. My grandparents also had a maid who lived in and had her own sitting-room next to the kitchen. My grandfather had a phenomenal knowledge of German history and used to take me for long walks in the park where he gave me lectures on the German royal houses, on great battles, on famous generals and their exploits. Although I was quite young I don't remember getting bored with these history lessons. My grandfather knew how to make them interesting for a young boy. Otherwise I remember seeing him at his typewriter and typing his letters or legal cases very slowly and deliberately. He wrote several legal commentaries. He also worried about his financial affairs. In the family we used to refer to his 'Hammer & Schmidt' nights. 'Hammer & Schmidt' were his bankers. At breakfast he used to complain about his sleepless nights when he worried about his finances, probably without any reason. They seemed to be quite comfortably off. My grandmother was a wonderful old lady, very gracious and generous. She lived for her husband and family. In the mornings, after a substantial breakfast, she would extricate her keys from her under-garments and open the big cupboard on the landing which was usually full to overflowing with provisions. She would then hand out to the maid what was required for the day's menu. It seemed a good life in those days.

We always went to Leipzig for Christmas. There was a big Christmas tree in the spacious salon and around it a number of tables. On them were our presents covered with a white cloth until the Christmas story had been read. Then the sheets were lifted and we rushed to our tables which usually overflowed with presents. On Christmas Eve either before or after the 'Bescherung' (the giving of the presents) we used to go to the Thomas Kirche, the famous old Church were J. S. Bach had been Kantor. We would hear the old Christmas Carols sung beautifully by the 'Thomaner Chor'. I think there used to be two or three services in succession because they were so popular. It was one of the highlights of our annual Christmas in Leipzig.

We also visited regularly my aunt, my father's sister, in Dresden. Usually, after celebrating Christmas in Leipzig, we used to go straight on to Dresden to be there for 'Sylvester' (New Year's Eve). My uncle there had also a senior post in the legal profession. They had two daughters, Inge and Baerbel, who were just slightly older than I. When midnight came and ushered in the New Year we would step out into the garden with our glasses of punch and watch the fireworks which were going off all over the city. Little did we guess then that fireworks of a different kind would years later destroy that beautiful city. I was born in Dresden. For a short time my father acted as legal adviser to a pharmaceutical firm in Dresden. The Chaplain of the Imperial Court who was a friend of my grandparents came to Dresden to baptise me. In those days it was quite customary for christenings to take place in the home. A few months after my birth we left Dresden. In 1925 my father was appointed judge at the local Court in Forst (in the District of the Lausitz). Forst was an industrial town south east of Berlin. It is on the Neisse which is now the official border with Poland and apparently today is quite an important frontier post. Forst could hardly be called an attractive town. It was full of cotton mills and had hundred of chimneys which belched out smoke all over the town. In those days one did not think about it, but today one would be very concerned about pollution. My parents found a flat on the third floor of a house in the Roonstrasse. We were on the edge of the town. From the back we could look out over open country. There we settled for the next 13 years and all my childhood was spent there.

Each morning my father went off to the Amtsgericht, the Court House, which was only a few minutes away. We had a fairly modest flat – a main bedroom, a dining room, a study, a spare room (which later became my room) and the kitchen and bathroom. For that small home we had a maid who lived in (she had a room in the attic). What she and my mother between them did all day I cannot imagine now. But everybody who could afford it had a maid. Ours was a young girl who came from the country and had to be trained. She was terribly homesick when she first came to us.

In due course I went to the Primary School. It was the custom that on the first school day each child was given a cone-shaped paperbag containing lots of sweets. I can still remember all these new school children converging on the school carrying their treasured bags. I soon made friends with quite a number of boys in my class. A dozen or more used to come to my birthday parties. As my birthday is on the longest day of the year these parties were usually out of doors, in the field behind our block of flats. We played football and other party games till late in the evening.

Next to the Court House where my father worked was the Turnhalle, the Sports Centre. Forst was known for two reasons – for its cotton factories and for its gymnasts. The Sports Club produced some outstanding gymnasts. Several of them were in the Olympic team at that time. We youngsters were very proud of them. The leader of the Club was an ex-Olympic gymnast and set a very high standard. My parents thought that it would be good for me to receive physical training and enrolled me in the Club. I used to go once a week after school and dreaded it because the training was quite demanding. My father used to work late most evenings and would drop in to watch me and then take me home. From time to time we used to give public displays in the only public hall in Forst. We used to rehearse our exercises for weeks before the event. In the summer we had some outdoor activities and we also had weekend camps somewhere in the country not far from home. As members of the Sports Club we wore blue uniforms. Herr Sachs was the tailor who made these uniforms. He was a member of the Olympic team and I had to go to him several times to be measured up. I was very proud to tell my schoolfriends that I had my uniform from him. I was a rather timid boy and I did not particularly enjoy the weekly drill, but I am sure it was good for me and my parents thought that it would stand me in good stead.

From the Primary School I went on to the Gymnasium which was a large building on the outskirts of the town. By now Hitler had come to power, in January 1933. I was really too young to understand the full significance of this ominous change. Suddenly there were swastikas flying from many buildings, columns of men in brown shirts and heavy boots looking like a paramilitary organization were marching through the streets. It all seemed to happen almost overnight. The economic situation in Germany had steadily deteriorated, unemployment was widespread. There was a general disillusionment with the parties in power. Along comes a party with high ideals, revolutionary zeal, big promises to reverse the downward spiral. No wonder that so many people fell for it and were prepared to give it the benefit of a doubt. I can still see pictures in the

papers showing the aged and dignified President von Hindenburg and the brash Adolf Hitler standing side by side at
Potsdam when Hitler became Chancellor. Those two men
seemed poles apart. Very quickly Hitler was in complete
control of Germany. In March 1933 the Nazis scored 43% of
the vote at the General Elections with the Socialists, Communists and Centre Party lagging well behind. By November of
that year all the other parties had been suppressed and the
Nazis won with 92%. The rest of the votes were invalid! that
was the end of democracy in Germany for the next 12 years.

Until 1935 life was relatively tolerable although it soon
became quite evident that the Nazis would pursue a militant
anti-semitic policy. As we were at least nominally a Christian
family we did not expect this policy to affect us personally.
Each summer we went on lovely holidays, always to the South
and to the mountains. My father was a keen mountaineer and
we used to go for long hikes and climbs, mainly in Austria and
the Tyrol. I remember a holiday in Mittenwald, not far from
Garmisch-Partenkirchen. Also a very hot summer near Bol-
zano. But the holiday I remember best was at Zell am See. We
went with my father's sister from Dresden and her two daughters (my uncle suffered severely from asthma and had to stay
at places which catered for his complaint). We rented a little
house right by the lake at Thumersbach from where we looked
right across to Zell on the other side of the lake. It was an
idyllic setting. From the house we could go straight into the
lake for our daily swim. It was also a good centre for walks
and excursions to some of the mountains surrounding us. It
was one of the last carefree holidays.

The countryside round Forst was also very beautiful with
extensive forests and some lakes and the river Neisse. My
father bought us all bicycles. At weekends and on public
holidays we would go off for the day with our picnic lunch
and explore the country. There was a favourite spot along the
Neisse where we went regularly in the summer to bathe. On
one occasion I was playing on my bike by the riverbank, lost
my balance and plunged head first with bicycle into the river.
As I had no spare clothes I had to cycle home like a drowned
rat. Not a very dignified sight!

The winters were usually very cold with snow and hard

frost. One part of the Sports Stadium was flooded in the winter months and became a public skating rink. We used to go skating there as often as time allowed. There was also a lake out in the country where I played ice hockey with my schoolfriends. After these bitterly cold outdoor activities it was a treat to come home and unfreeze by the heat of the tiled stove. There was, of course, no central heating in those days. Instead we had these solid stoves in the living rooms which were heated with brown coal. I think our bedrooms were unheated. We had double glazing to keep the worst of the cold out.

This rather enjoyable way of life changed after 1935. I seem to remember that at that time one day all the Jews in the town were forcibly marched through the streets. I think my father was spared that ordeal because he was not a Jew. But one of his fellow judges was subjected to that treatment. Very soon after that new laws were introduced according to which anybody of Jewish origin was declared 'non-aryan' and was liable to various restrictions and indignities. Sometime after 1935 my father was relieved of his office in Forst. He had just been transferred to Berlin for a trial period prior to being appointed to a senior post at a High Court there. This, of course, was ruled out now. In fact, at the prime of life, he suddenly found himself unemployed. This was the beginning of our trials and tribulations and as a boy of eleven I began to realise that our life would become more difficult and unpleasant. As far as I was concerned this did not affect me immediately. I had no problems at school, I had a number of friends, I still belonged to the Sports Club. One local businessman, a friend of my parents, offered my father some part-time work in his factory. He worked in the office and gained some experience in running a business. In fact, several families in the town, at some personal risk, proved very helpful during this time. At home, my father wrote a commentary on some legal matters. He had already been engaged in some writing before the Nazis came. But now he was no longer allowed to publish them in his own name. I remember that one commentary was eventually published under the name of his father-in-law. Another law which affected us directly was that Non-Aryans were no longer permitted to have living-in domestic help, but only women over forty-five. The reason given was that Jews were liable to abuse younger women sexually. It was all so petty and ludicrous and demeaning. It was a relentless policy which as the years went by became more and more disabling and destructive.

In the centre of the town, in the market square, stood the Protestant Parish Church. We used to go there from time to time. I went to the Sunday School. My mother as a Catholic went to her church, rather reluctantly because of a very rigid priest. During my last year in Forst I was prepared for Confirmation by the Parish Priest, Superintendent Kriebel, and a well meaning, but ineffectual deaconess. We were taken through the Catechism which we had to learn by heart and repeat parrot fashion. My father also went from time to time to Nossdorf, a little village out in the country. Not only the Jews, but also the Church suffered persecution from the Nazis. They had tried soon after 1933 to bring the Church under their influence. Many Christians compromised and the Church split virtually into three groups: The 'German' Christians who positively affirmed the new ideology; the Confessional Church which openly opposed Hitler; and the clergy and people in between who kept quiet and tried to keep out of the conflict. The Barmen Declaration of 1934 declared its rejection of the false new teaching and led to the formation of the Confessional Church with which men like Martin Niemoeller and Dietrich Bonhoeffer and the theologian Karl Barth were associated from the beginning. But so were many other pastors and congregations. And in course of time they remained the only active and public resistance to Hitler. Pastor Jacob at Nossdorf belonged to the Confessional Church. After 1945 he became one of the leading Bishops in the Lutheran Church in East Germany. Sometimes my father took me along to the Service there on a Sunday morning. In the Services we prayed for pastors who had recently been arrested, and for their families and congregations. We prayed for Paul Schneider who was arrested in May 1937 and spent most of his time in Buchenwald Concentration Camp (he died there in 1939). You could sense in those services that you were taking part in a demonstration against an evil regime. You also knew that you were in the presence of a pastor who was very courageous and took grave personal risks. He might not be there the following Sunday. Just another one to be removed from office and silenced.

I began to realise that there was some discrimination against me, too, when the Youth Section of the Sports Club was affiliated to the Hitler Youth. All groups or organisations for children and young people had to close down or come under the control of the Hitler Youth. But I was not allowed to be a member of it. And that meant that I could no longer join in some activities that my friends were involved in. I was different. From the time that I went to the Gymnasium I used to pick up one or two of my friends on the way to school. This went on for several years. Then suddenly these friends began to make some lame excuses why it was no longer convenient for me to call on them. I was too gullible to understand the reason, at least at the beginning. The parents probably advised their children not to mix with me. Or they were members of the Party and stirred things up. I began to discover that I was gradually being isolated. That was very hard for a child to accept.

The question has to be asked: Why did we not leave Germany at this stage when life became unpleasant and difficult? Some Jews emigrated soon after 1933 and certainly well before 1939. Well, there were several good reasons for hanging on. In the first place, you think twice and many more times before you decide to leave your own country and take the risk of starting a new life in a foreign country. It is a big step to take. And then you go on hoping that such an evil regime cannot last and will sooner or later be overthrown. And thirdly, unless one had a bank account in, say, Switzerland it was not easy to obtain entry into another country. Although Britain opened its doors to Jewish refugees one needed sponsors and permits. At that time our only contact in England was an aunt of my father's who lived in London. But she had limited means and could not provide the financial guarantee that was required. Moreover, there would have been the difficulty of finding a job for my father. As a German lawyer he would not have been qualified to practice in England. All these factors made us hesitate to consider emigration.

## 2

# Move to Dresden

ONE day in May 1938, quite out of the blue, my father had a severe heart attack. I still remember standing at the window of my parents' bedroom looking out for the doctor. It seemed like an eternity until he arrived. The Senior Physician of the local hospital was a friend of my parents. He rushed my father into the hospital regardless of what colleagues or staff might say. He was a brave man. He found my father a private room and looked after him. He was to us like an angel during this anxious time. Probably all the fears and anxieties and uncertainties had been building up. No work, no future, no dignity. This had come to a head now and caused this heart attack. Fortunately, he made a good recovery mainly due to the care of this doctor. In the summer we went to the wedding of my mother's sister (who was 21 years younger than my mother) in Muenster in Westphalia. By then, my father was well enough to come with us.

The illness was certainly one factor which prompted my parents to leave Forst. It was a small town, one was conspicuous and kept under scrutiny. With hindsight we probably should have moved when my father lost his job. But now in 1938 it was high time to move to a bigger city where we would be more anonymous. My parents felt drawn to Dresden, partly because they had briefly lived there before, partly because my aunt and her family lived there and partly because it was indeed a beautiful and stimulating city which had a great deal to offer. It is strange how events conspire. In late August my parents spent a few days in Dresden to explore the possibility of a move. My cousin Inge came from Dresden to look after me while my parents were away.

School term had just started again. One day coming back to the classroom after break I found written in large letters on the blackboard 'The Jew must go'. When the master came in he did not quite know how to handle it. I think he rebuked the class, but that was all. Needless to say I was too upset to stay.

I packed my bag, ran home and told my cousin. After lunch she took me to see the Deputy Head of the School at his home whom we knew quite well. His wife regretted that he was resting and could not be disturbed. Here was a typical example of the lack of moral courage. Ordinary, decent people were afraid to stand up and be counted. It might reflect badly on their Party record (most professional people were expected to be members of the Party) or their professional standing. Anyway, that nasty incident clinched my parents' decision to move to Dresden as quickly as possible. A day or two later I left Forst. I am told that I did not look back as the train pulled out of the station.

Fortunately, my parents found very quickly a pleasant and convenient flat on the top floor of a big Victorian house. It was quite near to my aunt's house and within walking distance of the Station and the City Centre. Within a fortnight we moved in and felt at once at home there. The next question was to find a school for me. Would anybody take me. My father took me to the Dreikoenigsschule on the banks of the Elbe. We went to see the headmaster, a man with a liberal outlook. He enquired about my background (by law I was graded a 'Mischling', i.e. half Aryan!). He brushed it aside and offered me a place in the school. This was quite a courageous decision on his part and it was, of course, a great relief to me and my parents. It was a very good school and it was the beginning of four very happy years there. Very quickly I made a number of friends. The few who survived the war are still my friends today.

Also in other respects the move to Dresden proved to be the right decision. We submerged in the big city. We saw a great deal of my aunt and her family and through them we met some of their friends who also became our friends. The local Church, the Lukaskirche, was just round the corner from us. We began to attend it. At that time Pfarrer Herrmann exercised an outstanding ministry there. He was a very powerful preacher and able teacher. His weekly Bible Lectures drew large numbers. I began to attend the Confirmation Class which he conducted. And living in a city of culture one was offered many attractions – the famous Picture Gallery, the equally famous Opera House, the good shopping centre, and many other amenities which we did not have before in a small town. It kept my father occupied. We could have been very contented in our new home and environment.

Suddenly, on 9th November, only a few weeks after our move to Dresden, another blow fell – the Kristallnacht. Triggered off by the assassination of a Nazi official in Paris by a Jew, synagogues all over Germany were burnt down and Jewish shops were looted and destroyed. I remember cycling to school next morning and seeing the smoking shell of the synagogue. That same afternoon in the main shopping street, the Prager Strasse, I saw a group of Jews being marched to the station. They had been rounded up and were probably on their way to a concentration camp. It was simply because we had only recently arrived in Dresden and our whereabouts were not yet known that my father escaped that fate. But this latest outrage was a sure signal for him to get out of Germany before it was too late. But how?

Several years earlier my parents had met Dudley Cheke. He had been a student and had stayed with a family in Forst to learn German. My parents had kept in loose touch with him. By now he was in the British Diplomatic Service and had just come back on home leave from his first posting in Mukden, Manchuria. After the events of the Kristallnacht he wrote to my father and offered his help. Here was indeed divine intervention. He was in a position to give the guarantee required by the British Government and sponsored my father so that he could obtain a three months' Visitors' Visa to England. It was a very hard decision for us as a family, but on the other hand there was no doubt in our minds that it was high time for my father to leave Germany before it was too late. Ideally, we would have preferred to go as a family. But that was not possible. My father needed to go first to explore the chances of finding some work to provide for us and also to look for a base for us and a school for me. Once that was arranged – and at the time we did not realise how difficult that was – we would follow him. We assumed that it would be only a temporary separation and that we would join him later in the year. The threat of a war did not occur to us in early 1939.

On 7th March 1939 my father left with two suitcases. He was only allowed to take with him German currency to the value of 10 shillings. When we saw him off at the station we did not realise that we would not see each other again for 6 or 7 years. At the end of that sad day of parting I wrote my first letter to him, the first of many over the next few years:

'It is now almost 12 hours since we said good bye to you. This brings you my first greetings as you arrive in England. And also my gratitude for your Confirmation present (I was to be confirmed 4 weeks later) – your life story which you have written for me. This will always remind me of you and I shall treasure it. I hope the crossing was good and that you are now with Mr Cheke (who was going to meet the boat at Southampton).'

A day or two after leaving us we had his first letter from Hamburg before he embarked on the 'Hansa'. With it came a very moving poem that he had written as a farewell to Germany and which is reproduced in his book *The Last Judgment*.

In one or two of our letters during that week we make veiled reference to the events of the previous days. We were very careful in all our correspondence not to make any direct comment on the political situation as one could never be quite sure if the letters were censored. The events referred to Hitler's occupation of Czechoslovakia. I mentioned in my letter that it had just been announced on the radio that all schools would have a day off to 'celebrate' what amounted to the rape of yet another country.

Our landlord was a Mr Mattersdorf. He and his wife lived on the ground floor. He was a banker and they were Jewish. In one of our first letters, soon after my father's departure, we wrote:

'The night before last we were called downstairs. Quite suddenly they have managed to get away. They worked right through two nights to get all their packing done. Yesterday morning they left for Leipzig and from there by air to Zurich. They both looked terrible.'

The next big event which sadly my father had to miss was my Confirmation at the beginning of April. The preparation for Confirmation is quite long and thorough in Germany. I had started it in Forst and had the last 6 months in Dresden. There were elaborate plans weeks before the day. The Confirmation is not only a religious, but also a social event. My grandparents came from Leipzig also two of my godparents came. The previous Sunday we, the candidates – we were about thirty – were examined during the main service in front of the congregation. We were all very nervous. My mother commented that we did not seem to be very 'clued up'. We were tongue-tied in front of such an intimidating audience. On the day itself which I think was Palm Sunday we all processed into St Luke's Church led by Pfarrer Herrmann. In the Lutheran Church the local Parish Priest confirms, not the Bishop. During the actual Confirmation we all knelt at the altar rail. As we were blessed we were each given a verse from the Bible as a kind of motto for the future. I am sure Herrmann must have thought very carefully about the choice of verses. When my turn came he gave me John 6. 68, 'Lord, to whom shall we go? You have the words of eternal life'. I am for ever grateful for that verse. It has been a guide and encouragement to me throughout my life and especially during the long war years when indeed I did not know where I was going and how it would all end.

After the service we all went back to our home. There was a splendid meal. My uncle Hans and my godfather Schoene made speeches. I was given many presents. We were all very conscious of my father's absence. Apart from that it was the last happy family reunion before the war.

By the second half of April my father had been in England for six weeks and his Visa was only valid for 3 months. If there was no work in sight for him by then he might have to return to Germany. We all realised that this would be a great risk and now both sides reluctantly raised this issue. There was the possibility of extending the Visa. I wrote to him about this time.

> 'It would be terribly hard for all three of us not to see each other again before long, but I am convinced that the circumstances demand that you stay. If you did return at the end of the 3 months none of us would feel easy. On the contrary, our fears would begin again. We feel much more at peace when we know that you are safe and well over there. Also if you return all the contacts you have made will come to nothing. I am afraid I can see no other option but this harsh reality.'

After all six weeks or even three months were a very short time to accomplish anything. Many refugees were trying to find a new existence for themselves and their families. In our desperation we had hoped that something would turn up quickly, but it stood to reason that it was bound to take time. After nearly four months in England going from one office to another, meeting various people, making applications there was still nothing to report. Every letter showed the strain of this uncertainty. We were concerned that my father had no means of his own. He just had some pocket money which kind friends gave him. His life was very austere. Fortunately he did not mind that as long as there was something at the end of the tunnel.

In the course of his many enquiries he had met the Bishop of Chichester, Dr George Bell. He had taken a particular interest in refugees from Germany. He was the President of the Refugee Committee of the British Churches. My father called there quite frequently and got to know the Bishop.

Just around the corner from us in Dresden we had two foreign Churches, the Russian Orthodox Church (which is still there) and a small Anglican Church serving the British community in Dresden. Before he left us my father used to go there from time to time and was quite attracted by the Anglican worship. When he came to England he put out feelers whether there were any openings for some kind of work in the Church of England. The Bishop took it up and made further enquiries. When we were on holiday in July we received the good news that he had been accepted for theological training. The Bishop had been instrumental in recommending him. This meant that at the age of fifty my father who had been a judge was going to begin again as a student on quite a different career.

We were, of course, overjoyed that at long last a new life was opening up for him and hopefully for us as well. Now we could at least begin to think in terms of joining him in England before very long. Provided, of course, that there was no war! Nobody wanted it, but the political tension was mounting all the time. In July my mother and I were on holiday in Austria. It is worth noting in passing that we had difficulties in finding accommodation. All the resorts were fully booked. And that only a few weeks before the outbreak of World War Two. The man in the street did not believe that Hitler would provoke a war with the other major powers.

My mother was planning to visit my father sometime in September or October. I was supposed to go as well, but my application for a passport was turned down. In any case, our plans were now overshadowed by the increasingly volatile political situation. On 24th August I wrote to my father:

> 'With every news item on Russia, Poland and Danzig I get a fright and think of you. Nobody can tell which way the pendulum will go. In these days and hours we pray that God may preserve us from a long separation. However much I long to have you here my mind tells me that we must be thankful that you are safely over there. I still hope that we shall all be spared the worst fears of this crisis.'

During the last days of August we were almost resigned to the inevitable. We wrote brief postcards to my father saying that we were trying to be brave and likewise we hoped that he would be given strength.

Years earlier when my mother was recovering from pneumonia in Switzerland she had met there a Swiss couple, the Georgs, and had kept in touch with them over the years. Frau Georg was a very fine Christian lady. She used to send us Bible texts in her own beautiful calligraphy. As it happened – and we thought providentially – Mr Georg's Christian name was the same as my father's – Werner. This turned out to be extremely useful during the war years. At the end of August my mother wrote to Frau Georg telling her that my father was now in England and that direct postal communications would certainly be cut off if war broke out. Would she drop a line to my father. This was the beginning of a fairly regular correspondence with my father via Switzerland. We were able to refer to 'Werner' as though we were talking about her husband. We were very fortunate that we had this lifeline right up to 1944 and it worked both ways. The only other communication was via the Red Cross in Geneva. One was allowed to write 25 words once a month on a special form. It took about six months to reach the other side by which time it was out of date.

I remember that terrible morning on 3rd September when war was declared and we knew that our hope of joining my father in England was now out of the question. Little did we know then what would happen to each one of us and that it would be years before we would see each other again. Initially life went on very much as before. We expected air-raids and military activity on the Western front, but there was very little of it. Everybody was still hopeful that one side or the other would step back from the abyss and that peace would be restored.

By the beginning of October my father had moved to Cambridge to begin his theological training. He had been offered a place at Cheshunt College, a Congregational College where the well known theologian John Whale was the Principal. We were relieved that in the circumstances my father was in a congenial setting and that his mind would be occupied with his studies. We kept in fairly regular touch with him via Switzerland. Our letters were opened and censored and we had to be very careful in what we wrote. But at least we knew that he was well and that he was surrounded by new friends and fellow students. We in turn also had the support of my aunt's family and a number of friends. But after 8th May 1940 things changed. I referred in my letter to this 'decisive and fateful day'. For on that day the war began in earnest and Hitler invaded the Low Countries and breached the Maginot Line.

There were no more letters from my father for the time being. We attributed this to the military operations. What, in fact, we did not realise and did not discover for some time was that on 12th May he was interned along with many other refugees of German nationality. They were first taken to a temporary camp near Liverpool where conditions were very primitive and then to a permanent camp at Douglas on the Isle of Man. They were only allowed to write 2 letters a week.

In July my father wrote to a friend in London, a Methodist Minister, from the camp:

> 'Though life behind barbed wire is not easy I must not complain knowing that this time is difficult for everybody. We all hope that this dark cloud will pass and that England will win the war. The worst of it is that we are not allowed to receive any news. Instead, there are many rumours going round the camp and nobody knows where they come from and if they are true. I try to make the best of this time which can be a good experience in the long run. Some of our friends have left for unknown

destinations (Canada ?), but some of the German pastors (among them Franz Hildebrandt, Niemoeller's former assistant in Berlin) are still here. We have morning and evening prayers and well attended services. As we are allowed to write only two letters a week I should be grateful if you would send this letter to Dr Whale (the Principal of his College).'

Part of the uncertainty of the internees was that they were afraid they would all be shipped to Canada and could be torpedoed by German U Boats on the way there.

We received the first direct note from him sometime in November. It had been written at the end of October. Letters that he had written to us previously never reached us. In that letter he said that he had taken a number of services in the camp, that there was a Bible Study Group, and that he was well and in good health. By the time we received this news it was already out of date.

At the beginning of the New Year (1941) we received a message via Switzerland written in November and from Cambridge. He was now at Ridley Hall, an Anglican evangelical college:

'You will be surprised to see my address. I am released and back at Cambridge and can continue my studies. It came quite suddenly, I could hardly believe I was free. It still feels like a miracle that I am no longer behind barbed wire and that I can walk without guards around me, that I can meet my old friends again, and especially that I can work. I owe this release to the Bishop of Chichester and to the Principal of my College. I know that you will rejoice with me about this news.'

Bishop Bell, according to his biography by Ronald Jasper (pp. 147–152), visited the camp twice and made urgent representations on behalf of the internees in the House of Lords. It must have been as a result of his interventions that my father was released. From now on we received again regular news once or twice a month. We also explored a Box number in Portugal through which, we were told, we could write to England. One day we received a summons from the Gestapo in Dresden. We went in fear and trembling to their Headquarters wondering what we had done. They had intercepted our letter and warned us not to use this address again. We were relieved that it was nothing worse.

Our life in Dresden continued to be surprisingly normal considering that there was a war raging in East and West. Right up to February 1945 Dresden was spared, probably the only major city in Germany that had not been the target of Allied air-raids. People from Berlin and as far away as Hamburg who had suffered from constant raids used to come to Dresden just to get a break and catch up on sleep. All the same, we were always on the alert for any possible attacks and had our regular air-raid warnings. One could ring a special telephone number where the flightpath of Allied bombers was monitored. At night I would also tune in from time to time to the BBC and avidly listen to their news. There was, of course, a severe penalty if you were caught, but the Nazis could not stop it and many people listened in the secrecy of their own homes. It gave one the feeling that one was not completely trapped by the Nazi propaganda machine.

1942 was an important year for me. In March I took my 'Abitur', the matriculation exams. At the end of the month was the school leaving ceremony and the presentation of the Matriculation Certificate. I had done quite well. I could look back on four happy years at the Dreikoenigsschule. There was the inevitable Nazi indoctrination which affected school assemblies and subjects like history. The syllabus had been rewritten to teach it from the point of view of Nazi ideology. But if one tried to ignore or resist this indoctrination one could still benefit from the teaching in general. I had made a number of good friends and one of the hardest things now was to say good bye to them. We had a farewell party which went on till the early hours of the morning. I recently passed the spot where the restaurant had stood where we held our party. It had probably been destroyed. But it brought back memories of that party. It marked the end of a fairly carefree youth for most of us. We dispersed into a hostile world and from now had to face the hardships and horrors of the war. Most of my friends were soon called up into the army and before long were caught up in the fighting, mainly on the Russian front. By the end of the war out of a class of over twenty only 6 or 7 were still alive. Quite a number had perished at Stalingrad.

For me it also meant a radical and immediate change. Under normal conditions I would have gone on to University, but I was not admitted. I was disqualified from joining the Forces. Before my father left us my parents had discussed my future and sought advice from some of their best friends. They had come to the conclusion that in the circumstances my best option was some kind of commercial training so that eventually I could find work in the export trade and work abroad. Well, obviously, that was not possible now. The only option open to me now was some training in industry which contributed to the war effort. So in April 1942, a few days after leaving school, I started work in an armaments factory, the Hille Werke. I was accepted as an apprentice.

The factory was on the outskirts of the city. We had to work 12 hours a day starting at 6 am with a short break for lunch. It meant getting up at 5 am every morning and coming home around 7 pm dead tired. The first six months I was employed on the factory floor. Looking back on it now I am glad I had to discover what that was like. But I disliked it intensely. I am not good with my hands, I was not interested in machines. Now I had to stand all day long turning some handle for a precision tool. I found it extremely boring and the day seemed very long. However, I was very fortunate. I had some super mates, older men with hearts of gold who were very understanding and patient with me and who, I think, appreciated my dilemma. The evenings and Sundays (we worked on Saturdays as well) were like oases in the wilderness. I relaxed and pursued my own interests. The first six months were the worst. After that I worked in the commercial departments of the factory and that work, though monotonous at times, was much more useful. This went on for two years. By now (1942/43) our correspondence with Switzerland became more sporadic. There was the occasional letter, more often just a postcard to say that we were alright. The mail between Switzerland and England was frequently suspended.

During this period my grandmother and my aunt (my father's sister Ilse) were deported to Theresienstadt in Czechoslovakia. My grandfather had mercifully died a year earlier in Berlin. Theresienstadt was, so to speak, the model camp to which Red Cross officials were taken to show them how 'humane' the treatment of the Jews by the Nazis was. I was reading recently that a well-known Jazz player, Coco Schu-

*In Forst 1928*

*Identity Card issued by Free French Forces at Marseille 1944*

mann, who was a Jew and who was one of the inmates there had to perform with some other musicians for a Nazi propaganda film. The macabre title of the film was 'The Fuehrer has donated a town to the Jews'. It was, in fact, a town that had been turned into a concentration camp. For the inmates – the elderly intellectuals, artists – it was an indignity and both mental and physical cruelty. My grandmother was in her eighties and was one of the kindest and gentlest ladies one could find anywhere. We assume that she must have died there in 1943. In our few remaining letters to Switzerland early in 1944 we mentioned that we had not heard anything from my aunt Ilse. She was probably taken to Auschwitz and perished there. After the war we gathered a little more about her fate. One of the survivors of Theresienstadt wrote to my father after the end of the war.

> 'When I arrived in Theresienstadt we were more than 40,000. This figure had decreased to 12,000 when we left due to deaths and further deportations. I obtained my information about your sister from a lady who shared a room with her. She was a social assistant and worked very hard last year (1944) in an asylum for very old people. She had been frequently ill. She should have been operated for appendicitis, but refused because of the danger of being too weak after the operation. Lack of food would have made recovery difficult. Since then she has been deported again, but there has been no further news.'

Sometime during these years – I can't remember when – my mother was officially declared a widow. The Nazis had tried to persuade my mother to divorce my father. When she refused they labelled my father as an absentee. Hence the new status for my mother and a widow's pension to go with it. As the war progressed we became more and more disheartened because we could not see an end to it and to Hitler's megalomanian rule. One way in which I tried to wrestle with the apparent hopelessness that engulfed us was to do some writing. Tschaikovsky's 'Pathetique' symphony which I had on records had made a great impression on me and spoke to my condition. There was also a verse from the Book of the Revelation which I found very uplifting 'Hold fast what you have so that no one may take away your crown' (3.11). I have no recollection now what the scenario of my writing was, but I can still see myself sitting in the garden on warm summer evenings after work and writing furiously. I think it was a story based on the third movement of the symphony, the triumphant march, and on the verse from Revelation. I wish I could see now what I wrote in those days, but it all perished in the flames.

By 1944 one was becoming aware that the situation both inside Germany and on both fronts was getting more and more precarious – more rationing, more and more people being conscripted, more reports of casualties. There were rumours that young people of my background would be called up for work in the occupied territories. One of my last messages via Switzerland was a postcard written the day before I left Dresden for forced labour (25th April):

> 'After these wonderful years here I have to say goodbye to my mother tomorrow. I am sure that the physical work will be good for me. We must all remain brave. Please don't worry about me. Yesterday and today I have been busy with farewells and preparations. Tomorrow morning I am off.'

I never saw my home in Dresden again. It was bombed and destroyed on Valentine's Day 1945. My mother was still there when the bombs began to fall on the night of 14th February. I found a brief report of her ordeal which she wrote some time afterwards. It tells what happened to her that night and in the weeks that followed:

> 'Our house was bombed while I and the other residents sheltered in the basement. We escaped from the burning house and together with many other survivors kept running until we reached the hills on the edge of the city. Amidst the noise of houses and walls collapsing one could hear the church bells which were set in motion by the firestorm. They sounded as if they were ringing for a funeral. And indeed it was a funeral, that of Dresden and of 200,000 of its inhabitants (probably less, estimates vary greatly). We spent the night in a small house crowded with survivors – crying children, old men and women, some soldiers, all totally exhausted. I was with a friend who had been in the shelter with me. The question for us both was now – where should we go from here? We clearly could not go back to the burning city. My husband was in England, my son somewhere in France, my parents had been bombed out in West Germany. I did not know where they lived. My friend suggested

I should go with her to Coburg where her parents lived. That town was 100 miles away. How could we get there? Trains were not running. There were no cars on the road. We could not get a lift. There was complete chaos. We had to walk.

Those whom we met on the road were refugees like us. It took us 12 days to get to our destination. The nights we spent mainly in the open air freezing. When we passed a house we were grateful when kind people gave us some milk or a piece of bread. Or they offered us a chair to sit down for a few hours. Finally, we reached Coburg, a lovely little town undamaged by the war. We were completely exhausted, unable to move another step. My friend's parents surrounded us with all their love and treated me like a daughter. I stayed with them for seven weeks, slowly recovering from the ordeal. It was a miracle that I had survived. Another miracle happened there. Out of the blue I received a postcard from my parents telling me that they had found a refuge in a small place in Saxony. They asked me to join them there. So I started another long journey. This time I was more fortunate. I managed to get lifts from the Red Cross and other transport quite often until I reached the village and was reunited with my parents.

It was not long before to our relief the Americans came and occupied the area. A kind American officer offered to put me in touch with my husband in England and let him know that I was alive. It took, of course, weeks until that contact was established. And it took more than another year (1946) when through the help of the Bishop of Chichester, Dr Bell, I was able to come to England. Looking back on that time now it seems like a dream or more like a nightmare, and yet it is true. It was a miracle that I survived all that I have written down here in a few words.'

# 3

# Forced Labour in France

EARLY April 1944 the rumours I mentioned in the last chapter were confirmed. I received my call-up papers, not for the German Army, but for the Organisation Todt. This was a kind of labour force which was set up by one of Hitler's Ministers and which operated in occupied territories as a back-up for the armed forces which by now were hard pressed. By the beginning of 1944 the war had at long last turned in favour of the Allies and the Nazis needed to mobilise extra manpower to sustain the war effort. Hence this labour force which was mainly deployed in Norway and in France, especially along the Atlantic Coast.

I had to report on the morning of 26th April at the Main Station with one suitcase. Destination unknown. I said goodbye to my mother at the tram stop near our home. I did not want her to come to the Station to see me off. It was a sad parting. Were we ever going to see each other again? My father in England, my mother in Germany, I about to leave for an unknown destination, and a world war in progress in which – as events proved – all three of us could have perished. I stood again at the same tram stop a short time ago, almost fifty years later. How much had happened in that time and how mercifully God had guided all three of us, especially during those turbulent events at the end of the war.

I arrived at the Station not knowing another soul. I was clearly very apprehensive and wondered who else would be in this convoy. I discovered that it was made up of cases like myself, i.e. 'semi-Aryans', political prisoners and men with criminal records. A very odd mixture of people, and quite clearly all of us fearful about the future. How would we be treated? Where would be land up? What would the work be like? Some said we were heading for Norway, others that we were being sent to France. Well, we were soon to find out! From the day we left Dresden I managed to keep a daily diary and by a stroke of good fortune I hung on to it through all the traumatic events of the next 15 months (which in retrospect seem more like 15 years). The memories of that time are based on notes that I jotted down each day. From time to time I shall quote verbatim what I scribbled down nearly fifty years ago.

In the afternoon of 26th April the train leaves Dresden with this motley collection of mainly young men. We pass Leipzig and it soon becomes clear that we are heading West. During the night we come through Frankfurt-on-Main and in the early hours of the morning we cross the frontier into France. I don't think any of us have much sleep that night in our anxiety to know where we are going. But next day it is quite obvious, in the afternoon we arrive in Paris. The leader in charge of our train load is an Italian. He does not seem to be very clear about the instructions that he has been given. We get lost and eventually stop somewhere in the city. We have another night with little sleep camping by the side of a Metro Station. Once or twice we have to go into the Station and take shelter because of air-raid warnings. Next morning coaches come and collect us and take us to the Todt Transit Camp on the periphery of Paris. There we kick our heels for the rest of the day while similar trainloads from other parts of Germany arrive. The next day we are registered and then the allocation to the various units is held. Rumours have it that most of us will be sent to the Atlantic Coast to reinforce the defences against a possible Allied invasion. Needless to say we are all very nervous wondering what our fate will be and what kind of unit we shall be in.

Here I have my first stroke of luck, or, as I interpreted it later, some divine providence. Of all the people to interview and allocate me it turns out that it is somebody I know. Or at least I had known him years earlier when we lived in Forst. Hanjo and I recognise each other and I relax because I know that he will want to be helpful. And so he is. Hanjo advises me confidentially that I should join one of the technical units. They would be deployed in the interior of France and would be less exposed to military action and harsh treatment. I have some anxious moments, so much depends on making the right move. I can't go away and think about it. I have to make up my mind there and then. Knowing Hanjo I am sure that I can rely on his advice. So I sign up for one of these technical units.

I wonder what would have happened to me had I been sent to the Atlantic Coast and had been caught up in the Allied invasion.

There are about twenty of us who have been allocated to one of these units. Later in the afternoon we are taken by coach to Bougival, one of the select suburbs of Paris. When we get there no proper accommodation has been arranged for us yet. For the moment we are put up in makeshift tents. The weather is already quite warm. We are surrounded by beautiful houses and gardens. It seems almost unreal to think that we are in a war and getting ready for action except for the frequent air-raid warnings.

To begin with there is not very much for us to do. We spend most of our time out in the open and get to know each other. The assignment of these 'technical' units is to equip 'emergency' trains which are mobile and can quickly be moved from A to B. They are labelled 'Katastrophen Einsatz', i.e. they will be deployed at strategic targets such as railway junctions which have been put out of action by air-raids and need to be cleared and made operational again. The technical skill required is fairly minimal. We shall be mainly a spade and shovel brigade!

First, these 'emergency' trains have to be equipped. Some basic railway carriages are in a siding near our camp. We spend the next fortnight installing them with sleeping quarters, a canteen, a storeroom, a toolroom, a place for the generator and all electrical equipment. The train will be our home for the next few months, we shall live and sleep there and use it as the base for our work. The electrical compartment turns out to be of special importance for me. I was rather amused when I was allocated to the technical outfit. As I have mentioned before I am not mechanically minded. But once again I am in luck. Among our mixed company I get to know early on another boy from Dresden, Henry Ball. We discover that we come from similar backgrounds and have quite a bit in common. As you will see in the following pages we soon become inseparable and share many risky experiences together. Unlike me Henry is very practical and is given the job of looking after the electrics on the train. Initially it means collecting all the gear – batteries, cable, tools, lights, etc. and wiring up the train. One day Henry asks me if I would like to be his mate. He needs another pair of hands and our boss says 'yes'. 'Hands' is the operative word. I know nothing about electrics, but I can hold a spanner and make myself generally useful. So begins our partnership.

Eventually the train is fully equipped and fitted out. On Sunday, 21st May we move in. Our boss is an Obertrupp-fuehrer and in Nazi uniform. My guess is that he is a mechanic in ordinary life. His job is to keep us in order and to deploy us. We settle into our new quarters and begin our nomadic existence. During the night a locomotive is attached to the train and at long last we set off. Once again the question in our minds – where are we going? The answer comes next morning when we arrive at an enormous railway junction on the outskirts of Orleans, called Les Aubrais. It is in an awful mess. It has recently undergone a heavy bombardment and the whole area looks like a landscape on the moon. Crater upon crater. Our job is to repair some of the damage so that essential traffic can get through again. Orleans is on a vital supply line to the front. It is, therefore, a prime target for air-raids. That means we are in the firing line, too. Not a pleasant thought. Our train is moved to one of the sidings in a little forest clearing at Cercottes, right on the edge of this railway junction. This now becomes our temporary home for the next few weeks.

It must have been a devastating raid. As we reconnoitre during the first few days in the direction of Orleans there is hardly anything intact for over two kilometers. The Allied bombers certainly succeeded in putting the transport system out of action. A number of goods trains lie crippled on the tracks with their supplies spilling out. There is an eerie silence. A once busy station is completely immobilised. Very quickly we are put to work. A large number of local people have been conscripted as well. Among the workforce we can spot one or two priests in their soutanes wielding a spade. The first job is to fill in the bomb craters and level the ground. Then the railway workers move in and put the sleepers in place and then fix and align the rails. It is impossible to repair the whole damage. The priority is to open up one or two tracks to let essential traffic through again.

Apparently a troop transport was caught in the raid and a number of soldiers were killed. In the process of digging we find the remains of several German soldiers. They have been completely submerged under the craters. We carry their bodies to the local cemetery. Local people who pass us raise their hats or make the sign of the cross, even for their enemies.

One night there is more than the usual activity in the air. We have several alarms. Next morning we are not surprised to learn through the grapevine that the Allied Forces have landed on the Cherbourg Peninsular. This is the news we have all been waiting for. We are very excited. It is, of course, too early to rejoice. We have to wait and see whether the invasion will succeed. But at long last there is at least the hope that the liberation of France and of Europe has begun. And that would mean our liberation, too. There is plenty of speculation among us how long it will take before we are free. The chance to escape which we cherish secretly is now more likely. We go to bed that night with wishful thinking about the future. However, there will be several nightmares before our dreams are fulfilled.

Indirectly, the invasion gives us our baptism by fire. Suddenly at lunchtime an American fighter appears out of the sky and swoops down on our train. Its machine gun fire hits our water carrier. Luckily there are no casualties and no other damage. Two days later, we have our first proper raid. 100 bombers flying in immaculate formation drop their deadly bombs at either end of Les Aubrais. They seem to be complete masters of the sky. There are no anti aircraft guns to protect us. Fortunately, we are not in the actual target area, but it is quite unnerving to look up and see the bombs hurtling down. As soon as the raid is over we are moved to the section were the bombs have wrought havoc.

Two nights later we have another heavy raid on Les Aubrais. The Allies are clearly determined to dislocate the transport system and stop the Germans from rushing fresh supplies to the front. We suddenly wake up in the middle of the night and see the whole sky lit up with marker lights. We rush out of the train at the last moment and throw ourselves down in the wood next to the clearing as the bombs begin to rain down on us. This goes on for about half an hour, but seems like eternity. We are without any shelter, but mercifully none of the bombs fall near the train and we are alright. We gather ourselves together and await the dawn to survey the damage. All our work has been undone and we go back next morning to start all over again. It is quite demoralising. And now there is a new peril. Some of the bombs have delayed action fuses. During the next two or three days they go off without warning. Several of the local people working alongside us are killed or maimed. It is a most uncomfortable feeling digging among the debris and wondering whether at any moment a bomb will explode underneath us. We also decide to sleep in the wood for the next few days as we might well have more raids. It is now June. The weather is warm and sleeping out in the open is no hardship.

During these weeks after the invasion there is increased air activity. Many times our work on the site is interrupted by air-raid warnings. Day after day we watch heavy bombers passing overhead in prefect formation flanked by fighters which look like little watchdogs and circle round them. Most of the time they are on their way to other targets, probably inside Germany. There are no signs of the German airforce. They are probably preoccupied trying to stop the advance of the invading Allies.

The general spirit in our unit is fairly good. The Obertrupp-fuehrer is the typical minor Nazi official. On the whole we get on with him and he is quite reasonable as long as we get on with our work. However, we raise our eyebrows when one day he returns from Paris with a red haired female in tow. She moves in with him and organises us as well. This must be against the rules, but who cares. No official ever comes near us to check up on us or on our boss. Among ourselves we make the best of an odd situation. We come from very different backgrounds, but our common fate has thrown us together. Some of the others have horrific stories to tell of their treatment by the Nazis. My closest ally is, of course, Henry. I remember a nice chap from Bremen. There are two characters from Berlin. We shall hear of Otto later. Then there is Leo from Alsace. He is an older man, an engineer. He speaks French fluently which later will prove a great asset. And there is another Leo and Walter, both from Austria. Again we shall hear more of them. Walter looks the typical Hitler Youth with very fair hair, but he also comes from a non-Aryan background. There are the inevitable frictions and quarrels among us from time to time. That is bound to happen when we are very much on top of one another. But we realise that whether we like each other or not we have to keep on good terms to make life bearable.

At the beginning of July I record another heavy raid in the early hours of the morning. This time we get enough warning to take shelter in the woods. But two bombs just miss our train. In the morning we look around to assess the damage. All our work of the past few weeks has been virtually undone once again. The whole station is devastated as though a huge plough has turned everything upside down. When some bombs go off not very far from us we beat a hasty retreat. We take a look at an American bomber which had crashed quite close to us during the raid.

Once again we start to dig and fill in the craters and disentangle twisted rails. And all the time we have to be on the alert for more delayed action explosives. We are told that normally they tend to be safe after 72 hours. But I record that four days later another six bombs blow up, one only 150 metres from where we are working. The next day we are pulled out from that section because another huge explosion showers us with earth and stones. In between this work on the site I stay behind in the train and assist Henry with any electrical jobs that need doing.

One day I am called to the Obertruppfuehrer. I wonder what I have done. But the reason is that Franz who has acted as clerk for our unit is sent back to headquarters for some disciplinary reason. I am now given his job. I am responsible for the day to day running of the unit. It means ordering our supplies, handing out the food, keeping the accounts. It also means that I stay in the train and don't work on the site. I am given a certain amount of liberty which is very welcome. I have to collect some of the supplies and can get out into the town from time to time. That gives me the opportunity to escape. But in a country still occupied by the Germans and without any link to the Underground Movement it would prove quite difficult. I also have some of the others to consider.

I prefer to wait for a suitable moment when Henry and I and perhaps a few of the others can break out together.

Suddenly, one day in the middle of July, we are told that we have been given orders to move on. We are quite glad to leave Les Aubrais. It is a prime target for the Allies and we are rather exposed there. But would our next assignment be any safer? Our next port of call is Etampes, nearer Paris. The station itself is still intact, but our unit will be put to work some 10 kilometres down the line where the track has been bombed and the line is completely blocked.

Then we hear the news that there has been an attempt on Hitler's life at his Headquarters in the East, but that apparently he has been only slightly injured. To this day it is still a mystery to me why this coup failed. Had it succeeded, the war would probably have ended sooner, much innocent suffering and death could have been prevented and the Nazi regime might have been overthrown by opposition inside Germany. Instead that opposition which was badly co-ordinated was now ruthlessly prosecuted, tortured, tried and eliminated. Hundreds of able and potential political and military leaders who could have played an important role in a future Germany perished. Instead the war went on with increasing intensity for another year. On a purely human level I have always found it a theological stumbling block why God did not allow this coup to succeed. It was such a near thing. But then God has given us our freedom of action and does not intervene directly in our affairs. And we must accept that there are many things in this complex world which we just do not understand and we have to live with these mysteries.

We don't stay long in Etampes. After a week or so the line has been cleared. At the beginning of August we are on the move again. We only move a short distance in the direction of Dijon. Not far from Dourdan a trainload of petrol tankers has been attacked and blown up. The railway track is littered with thousands of burnt-out canisters. They are still partly smouldering. It must have been a fearful explosion when it happened. Once again we are put to work to clear up this mess.

For the first time I record that the Allied forces are actually advancing in our direction. We know that the invasion has succeeded. We can see that there is increasing air activity, we are told that the Resistance is more active. But now for the first time we hear that the Allied advance is gathering momentum. There are rumours that the Americans are only 45 kilometres away, that they are approaching Orleans, that we are going to be pulled back. We think that in the distance we can hear artillery fire. Within a matter of a few days a kind of panic sets in. Needless to say we are beginning to wonder what will happen to us. Three of us are sent off to the nearest depot where we get our food supplies. When we get there the place is in total confusion. They are feverishly loading up. We are firmly told by the officer in charge that there are no supplies for us 'B-Germans' (we were regarded as inferior). We return empty handed. Transport is virtually non-existent. We walk part of the way home, then get a lift on a locomotive which is going in our direction. Finally, with a bit of luck we meet up with our train which had been moved again.

We are shunted backwards and forwards. The situation changes almost from hour to hour. There are several air-raids on stations around us. We are moved to another site where a transport has been attacked and blocks the line. But before we have time to get that problem sorted out there is more panic that evening. The Americans are said to be within 20 kilometres. We are attached to another train and pulled out in the direction of Dijon. Is this the moment for us to make our bid for freedom? There are five of us who have been talking about it secretly – Henry and I, Leo from Alsace, and the two Austrians, Leo and Walter. We have a heated debate and consider the pros and cons, but in the end decide that it is not yet the right moment. There is so much at stake.

At one point a locomotive runs into the back of our train and causes havoc. Then we suddenly stop because the line in front of us has been bombed. In the middle of the night there is an almighty explosion. The retreating Germany army has probably blown up one of their ammunition depots. The whole sky is lit up. Eventually the line is cleared and we press on. This succession of trains, all trying to get out, presents a convenient target for the fighter-bombers. We are on constant alert.

Late that evening we arrive in Dijon and are shunted to one

of the sidings. We discover that we have a spy in the camp.
A chap called Ritter is in league with the Obertruppfuehrer
and keeps a good eye on us. They have probably twigged
that we are up to something. We have to be very careful.
The whole unit is in a state of heightened tension because of
the gathering threat of the Allied advance. While we are in
Dijon we hear that Paris has fallen (2nd August). A historic
date. It can't be long now for the Allies to catch up with us.

The following day we are on the move again. There are
orders and counter-orders. We get to a little town called Dole,
some 50 kilometers away. But the next day we are ordered
back to Dijon, only to find that the order is cancelled at the
last minute because Dijon is choked with trains all trying to
get out before it is too late. There is a general feeling that
rapidly the situation is getting out of control.

On Saturday, 26th August we find ourselves on the way to
Dijon again. At Auxonne we are diverted to a minor line and
come to a village, Lamarche. Here we are really off the
beaten track. We hear that the Resistance is quite active here
and is practically in control of this rural area. We should
have been given an armed guard at Auxonne. But perhaps it
is just as well we are without it. We don't want to be identified with the Wehrmacht. Our job is to raise a locomotive.
The Resistance have uncoupled the rails and the locomotive
has toppled over. During the night we take it in turn to
keep watch in case we are being attacked by the local Resistance. This is where Leo, our French speaker, proves his
worth. He has a word with the station master and explains
to him who we are. Perhaps that is the reason why the
Resistance leave us alone. When our job is finished we are
pulled back to Auxonne. There we find a hive of activity.
Several labour batallions are digging trenches. The German
High Command is trying to set up a new defence line to hold
up the Allied advance, but we doubt whether anything will
stop them now.

At the beginning of September we are once again in Dijon.
We hear that there is now only one route open to get out and
back to Germany. We see one train after another leaving filled
to overflowing with troops, railway personnel, the wounded,
some women and children. Their morale is very low. We can

tell from talking to some of them. They can't see any sense in
fighting any longer. There are some pathetic sights – soldiers
in shorts or trousers. No proper uniform. They have lost
everything and have just escaped capture. Some hobble along
on sticks. The sight of a defeated army! Whether they will all
get out before they are cut off is a big question. It is also a
question which exercises us.

We are informed that we shall be pulled out via Gray-
Belfort and then towards the German border. French railway
workers go on strike and make the transport system even
more chaotic. We are being promised a locomotive the next
day. We wait all day, eventually it arrives. We feel all very
tense. We can only travel by night because of the constant
danger of air attacks. We are the eighth and last train to
leave. The five of us discuss secretly our chances of escape.
We know how much is at stake and we know very well that
if we are caught in the act we shall probably be shot on the
spot. On the other hand we do not want to go back to
Germany because we can't tell what would happen to us
there. We organise our few belongings, just one bag each, so
that we can make our get-away at a moment's notice. But
we have to be on our guard because we are being watched.

On Tuesday, 7th September we depart via Lamarche-Genlis.
It will be a red letter day for us. We make very slow progress,
constant stopping and starting. We hear that Besancon has
been taken by the Allies and that the chances of getting
through are slim. At dusk we arrive at Gray station. While the
train is stationary just outside the station, in the gathering
darkness, we decide to go. At 9.45 pm – it is almost dark – the
five of us silently drop from the train, race down the embank-
ment and disappear in the undergrowth. A moment later the
train moves on. But then it stops again. Our escape has
probably been discovered. The whole areas is suddenly lit up
with coloured flares. Will they come after us? A few critical
and anxious moments. We push on into the woods and hide in
the thick undergrowth. A few minutes later the train gathers
speed and disappears. They can't really afford to be held up
and look for us. We are left to our fate. And suddenly we are
free, the first time for over 11 years! We can hardly believe it.
And this is not the moment to indulge in our freedom. We are

not yet out of the wood, so to speak. There are more immediate obstacles to bridge before we can be sure we are safe and free. And how sure can we be? The next few months will tell . . .

# 4

# First Taste of Freedom

IN our daydreams we had hoped that we would walk straight into the local Resistance and that they would welcome us with open arms. That, I am afraid, does not happen. In fact, beyond that initial leap from the train we really had no idea what would happen next. We had taken the first steps towards freedom, but the first night of it does not feel like it at all. It is most uncomfortable. We take refuge in the small wood not far from the station. By the time the train has disappeared into the distance and we emerge from the undergrowth it is pitch dark. We don't know where we are, we can hardly see anything. We dare not explore our surroundings. The only sensible thing is to stay put and spend the night there in the open air. It is only the beginning of September, but there is already quite a nip in the air. We are still shivering with all the excitement of our escape. But on top of that we are frozen with the cold night air. It is impossible to sleep. Added to the physical discomfort is the apprehension of the unknown. What will the next day bring? Although the German army is in retreat some of their rearguard units are still around and obviously we must steer clear of them. It is a long night while we wait for the dawn.

Next morning we leave our bags hidden in the undergrowth. We want to look as inconspicuous as possible and don't want to be cluttered up with our few belongings while we look for proper shelter. Sure enough, when we step out of the wood we spot a column of army trucks in the first village we approach. We make a bee-line round it and keep well out of view. Eventually we come to a little cottage which belongs to a forestry worker. He directs us to a little hamlet just down the road. We knock on the first door we come to and explain in our halting French (unfortunately we lost Leo, our interpreter, in the dark during the escape) who we are and that we are looking for the Resistance. They can probably tell from our faces that we are still in a state of shock and that we are desperately looking for a safe hiding place. They seem to trust us and offer us shelter in their barn. We murmur our thanks and just flop in the hay. By now we are completely exhausted after a sleepless night and all the stress of the preceding days. In minutes we are fast asleep and surface very much later in the day. We must have been beyond caring that these folk would not betray us.

The news of our arrival has spread quickly in this hamlet. When we awake a charming couple appear in the barn to take a close look at us. They are from Paris and have a small place down here. They have come down before Paris was liberated to take refuge in the country. Their name is Marchant-Hacot. We tell them a little more about ourselves and they seem to trust us. We are invited to their home and given a wonderful meal, the best we have had for a long time. All through the evening other folk from the village drop in and bring us something – milk, apples, bread. We are treated like VIPs. It all seems like a dream. For the first time we feel safe and among friends who want to spoil us. We go to bed that night in our barn overwhelmed by human kindness and compassion.

Again, the next day different kind people entertain us and look after our needs. One of the local men goes back with us to the wood outside Gray station to recover our bags. The whole village goes out of their way to make us feel at home. However, we are not yet out of danger. The next morning they wake us and urge us to clear out quickly. Some straggling German units are still passing through. We forget that the villagers are at risk, too. If we are caught there they will be held to ransom. We disappear straightaway and hide in the adjacent woods. Every so often somebody from the hamlet turns up and brings us something to eat and keeps us informed. In the distance we can hear the noise of cars and horses, many commandeered locally by the Germans for their retreat. It is another tense and uncomfortable day for us. As long as there are still remnants of the Nazis around we cannot feel completely safe.

All that changes on the following day. The last German troops leave in the direction of Belfort. In the afternoon somebody comes running to our hiding place to tell us that the Americans have entered Gray and that the area has been liberated (in fact, we learn later that it was not the American

Army, but the Free French Forces who moved into the town).
We come out of our shelter and move back into the barn. We
join the folk at the Chapelotte (the name of the hamlet) in
their joy that their hour of freedom has come at long last.

Later that day we have another great joy. Leo, our French
speaking member, whom we had lost in the dark when we
escaped turns up. Great relief all round. He has been looking
for us. Fortunately news travels quickly and he has heard that
a group of four young men had turned up at this hamlet. In
the meantime Leo has found a place in Gray and there is room
for us, too. So we gather our few belongings. We say our
goodbyes to our kind hosts who at some risk have given us
shelter. We promise to come back again to see them. But now
we move with Leo to Gray. It is important that one of us
speaks French and can act as our interpreter and spokesman.
No doubt we shall have to report to the local authorities and
identify ourselves. We find the town in a state of great excitement. The French tricolore, so long hidden, is flying everywhere and the whole town has turned out to celebrate their
freedom. We receive another warm welcome from our new
hosts. That night, for the first time in ages, we sink into the
most comfortable feather beds. The long ordeal seems to be
over. Along with all the other happy people around us we are
free. Or at least we think we are. In our simplicity we imagine
that once we have been recognised for what we are, victims of
Nazi oppression, we shall be given special treatment and
either repatriated after the collapse of Germany or – as in my
case – given special facilities to go to England and join my
father. It might take a little while to organise this in the
present chaos, but surely it would be only a matter of time. In
the meantime the French are bound to treat us well. There is
no doubt in my mind that God is with us and that all will be
well now. This could then be the end of the story, but I am
afraid it is not. In fact, it is only the next instalment of our
adventures, with many more to come. Very quickly we shall
be brought down to earth and made to realise that things are
not quite as simple and straightforward as we had imagined
them to be.

Next day, after a good night's sleep, we join again the
celebrations. We witness the most bizarre scenes. Girls who

had fraternised with German soldiers have their heads shaved in public and are dragged through the streets with derisive shouts of 'shame' from the onlookers. Not a pretty sight, but one can understand it. Bitterness and anger have built up over a long period of the Nazi occupation and now, in the hour of liberation, the bubble bursts. At long last people can give vent to their pent-up emotions. Later that day there are more shouts, of a very different kind, when the local Resistance units march through the town in a great victory parade. And here we are – this group of Germans, also just liberated – in the midst of this jubilant crowd sharing in their celebration. Our friends from the Chapelotte have also come over to Gray to join in the festivities. We meet up with them and share a drink together. It is a memorable day and, as we then think, the beginning of a new life for us.

However, as it happens so often in life, this joy is shortlived. One moment we have everything going for us, the next it turns into the opposite. Our friends at the Chapelotte have invited us for lunch and the next morning we return there. On the way we are suddenly aware that there are people behind us and trying to catch up with us. They stop us and point their guns at us. They are members of the Resistance who suspect us and now arrest us. Instead of a happy lunch at the Chapelotte we are driven back to the Gendarmerie at Gray and locked up in a dark cell. What a sudden terrible and totally unexpected reversal of our fortunes! We had fondly imagined that the French Resistance would receive us with open arms. Instead we are treated as enemies and put behind lock and key. We still think there must be a mistake and that once we have had a chance of explaining properly who we are we shall be set free again.

Later we are taken to the military barracks. There we are subjected to a thorough body search and then locked up in a cell for the night. We find that we are not the only 'prisoners'. There are one or two Poles and several other Central Europeans. Like us they must have escaped from the German Labour batallions and had been picked up by the Resistance. We try to go to sleep on the hard floor with hardly a covering of straw and the nights are getting chilly now. And our minds are over-active. We can't understand why fate should have struck such a cruel blow just when we thought that everything was in our favour. We wonder what will happen to us now.

In the morning we are taken to the captain of the local Resistance. To our great relief, he seems a pleasant and reasonable man. He listens carefully to our story. Our spirits revive. Leo, our friend from Alsace, is released straightaway. The rest of us are technically interned for the time being. Looking at it dispassionately, the French must be in a dilemma to know how to treat us. We have been in the employ of the Germans. How can they be sure that our story is true. We cannot prove it. And in these early days of the liberation there is still a great deal of confusion. All kinds of people of different nationalities are roaming the countryside. From their point of view it is safer to keep us under surveillance than to let us go. From our point of view that is hard to understand. We feel that we have a right to be free. But we are at their mercy. For the moment we are given two rooms in the barracks and allowed to move freely within the confines of this place. And we are given the same food as the members of the Resistance. By our standards that is very good and we can't grumble.

The next few days are very trying. There is nothing for us to do. We sit around, we talk about out future, we look out of the window, we walk round the square to get some exercise and fresh air. In another part of the barracks we can observe German prisoners, about 150 of them. They are a pathetic sight. They look defeated and demoralised. Compared with them we are quite fortunate. We are not prisoners, or at least we think we are a different species, and will be treated accordingly. There is one piece of news that cheers us up. Leo from Alsace who is still in Gray comes to see us. He has heard that our train has been totally destroyed in an air attack near Vesoul, not far from Gray. If the rumour is true – and retreating trains were tempting targets – it is an added confirmation that it was right to escape when we did. Had we stayed on we might well be dead now. We wonder what will have happened to the other members of the unit.

During the next few days our fortunes go up and down. The truth is that the French just do not know how to deal with us. We are neither fish nor fowl. And in any case, they have more important things to worry about. We are not a priority for

them. One day they decide to attach us to a Polish unit. There
are quite a number of Poles who have absconded from the
Germans. Along with them we are going to be employed on
guard duty: at the civilian prison, at the hospital where
wounded German POWs are being treated, at the main gates
of the barracks. We have a certain degree of freedom and we
have something to keep us occupied. This goes on for several
days.

One day we are not given any duties and we begin to
wonder what the reason might be. We soon find out. We are
suddenly told to stay in our rooms and to regard ourselves as
prisoners. We don't know where we are. One moment we
guard other prisoners, the next we are prisoners ourselves. The
reason seems to be that there is now a rather fanatical officer
in charge who distrusts us and has decided to clamp down on
our status. We protest. We argue that we are a special case
and cannot be treated as prisoners. But we remain confined to
barracks. Once again we kick our heels. There are rumours
that we are going to be moved to Besancon. If this is the case
the decision about our fate will be passed on to somebody else.

It is now mid-October. One day we are given orders to get
ourselves ready. We are herded together in two lorries, about
100 of us, mainly Poles. We are moved to the army barracks in
Besancon. This time it is a strict prison regime. We are
guarded by French soldiers from Senegal who stand on duty
outside our room with fixed bayonets. They even take us to
the toilets. This is very depressing for us and the very opposite
to what we had expected when we escaped. But as the days go
by we make friends with our guards and they relax their
watch.

After a few days a chap turns up who calls himself a Jewish
adviser. He looks in several times and makes vague promises
that the Jewish Committee in the town will intervene for us.
Later we suspect that he appeared in that guise to sound us
out and to see whether we were genuine. We are also told that
the authorities are investigating our case and that we shall
hear soon what they decide about our fate. Meanwhile we
stand and stare all day and get very fed up with nothing to do.
What makes things worse is the weather which is now damp
and cold. We shiver in our threadbare clothes. We talk to the

sergeant on duty and complain that we are just sitting around and nobody seems to care what is happening to us. His reply is that we should consider ourselves lucky to be out of the clutches of the Nazis. The authorities have far more important and urgent matters to sort out. We are just small fish in a large pond. At least we are safe, we have a roof over our heads, we have food and drink. We shall probably be moved on before long. He advises us to calm down and make the best of the situation. It is very demoralising for us.

By now we have become a mixed bag of humanity who have appeared from the four winds of heaven and have been picked up by the French – Poles, Russians, Yugoslavs, Czechs. The barracks have become a transit camp for this odd collection of refugees. Like us they had been conscripted by the Nazis and had also managed to escape during the general confusion of the German retreat. There are rumours that we shall all be transferred to Marseille. There are apparently repatriation camps down there for the various nationalities. We feel that would be at least better than kicking our heels in Besancon. But would there be a repatriation camp for Germans as well? We doubt it.

On 11th October we are told to prepare for a move the following day. Forty of us are herded together in a cattle truck and each of the trucks has a guard from the FFI (Free French Forces). Most of the others in our wagon are Russians. The smell is unbearable. We can hardly breathe. There is not enough room for everybody to sit on the bare boards. Sleep is quite impossible. Life in our emergency train seemed a luxury compared with this. Late that evening we arrive in Dijon. We seem to have been here before!

In the morning they let us out to urinate. Then back again. Later I have a chance to catch sight of the officer in charge of the transport and complain about the intolerable conditions. He is sympathetic. He seems to know about us and will see what he can do. To our great relief we are moved to another wagon full of Yugoslavs. But there is more space and we are no longer locked up and under guard. We are allowed out for a breather whenever there is a stop on our long journey down south.

The railway system is still in chaos, many hold-ups and

diversions. We are making very slow progress. We are heading in the direction of Lyon, but there are repairs on the line. We are diverted and proceed in a roundabout way down south. Eventually we arrive in Lyon one evening, and are shunted to a siding. We are told that we shall probably be held up there for some time before we move on to Marseille.

We have had hardly any food on the way and are starving hungry. We explore our surroundings and find a little restaurant quite close to the station. There are three of us. We can do with a meal. It is a far better way to spend the evening than to sit on the bare boards of the cattle truck. And we are not likely to move on before the morning at the earliest. We order some food. We celebrate our meal with a bottle of local wine. A rare treat. Suddenly in the middle of the meal one of the Yugoslavs from our wagon rushes in. We are to return at once. The train will leave any moment. It takes a few minutes to settle our bill. We have to leave the rest of the food and rush back to the station. By now it is pitch dark. We try to find the train where we had left it. It has gone. We make frantic enquiries and are told that the train had left. Unexpectedly the line was cleared and the transport was able to resume its journey. We must have missed it by a few minutes. But we have been left behind. I feel absolutely desolate. What are we to do? My few belongings are in the train, so are my friends. I feel completely deserted in the middle of France. And I can only blame myself for this stupidity. Why did I go off in search of something to eat instead of keeping close to the train? But it is no use regretting my carelessness now. The train is heading south and we are left behind in Lyon. What a terrible turn of events.

The three of us hold a brief council of war. We clamber across the tracks to the station. A fast train to Marseille stands on the platform and is about to depart. We have only a few francs on us and can't afford the fare to Marseille. At the last minute we just jump aboard the train and we are on our way. The train is crowded with people, but we find a space in the gangway. By now it is about midnight. Our faint hope is that we might catch up with our transport somewhere along the line or locate it when we get to Marseille. I still feel numb with fear. If somebody notices that we are foreigners we are in trouble. We possess no identity papers, nothing that would protect us if we are caught. For the moment I just flop on the floor of the gangway and shut my eyes.

Monday 16th October dawns. We stand at the window and look out on the beautiful countryside of the Provence. We pass through Avignon. It could be such a pleasant journey. But all the time there is the nagging question 'What will happen next?' And the question becomes more pressing when the ticket collector comes through the train. We have no tickets, no identification, no money, no proper French to explain our dilemma. And nobody would believe us. I feel desperate. The collector moves from compartment to compartment. Any moment it is our turn and then we are caught. Help! Just then the train stops at one of the stations. The collector gets out and does not come back. The timing is uncanny. We are let off for the moment and we are left in peace for the rest of the journey.

# 5

# From Foreign Legion to 'Free Germany'

In the early morning we arrive in Marseille. Our apprehension is at fever pitch. Will we find our transport here? If not, what do we do in a strange city where we do not know a soul? One of our threesome has already left us. He jumped out at one of the stations on the way. That leaves Otto and me. Otto is a typical Berliner, ever bright and breezy. He is probably a bit of a crook. Somehow we find a back exit and manage to get out of the station without having to produce a ticket. Otto says good-bye to me. He will try his luck to find some work. That leaves me in the middle of this bustling city without a clue where to go.

From the moment I escaped the thought that was uppermost in my mind had been to make contact with my father in London. I wrote a postcard from Gray which I asked Leo to post, but I was doubtful whether it would ever reach him. I had no desire to go back to Germany even if that opportunity arose. I wanted to go to England and be reunited with my father. So my first step must be to try and make that initial contact. With that in mind and for want of anything else to do I decide to find the British Consulate. I am naive enough to think that they will give me a hearing and perhaps temporarily provide me with shelter. What I have failed to realise is that France has only just been liberated and the British have not yet returned to their diplomatic posts. When I eventually find the Consulate it is still administered by the Swiss. There is no sympathetic British official waiting for me. Instead I meet a suspicious French secretary at the Reception Desk. I present my case and my connection with England. Alas, he shows no interest or compassion at all and points out in a very matter of fact voice that I am still a German citizen. The Consulate can't help me. Deflated and rebuffed I come out and wonder where I can look for help.

Before we left the station we tried to find out whether there was any information about our transport. It must have arrived in Marseille in the early hours of the morning unless it had been held up somewhere. Nobody seems to know anything about it. What about contacting the FFI (Free French Forces) who had organised the convoy and might know its where-abouts. I make my way to their headquarters and in fear and trembling call there. To begin with I meet a fairly hostile reception and wonder whether I have walked into the lion's den. Their first reaction is to treat me as a prisoner of war. But after some more pleading they relent and send me off with a very pleasant sergeant to make enquiries about the convoy. If we can track it down I have proved my case. But that is like looking for a needle in a haystack in a big teaming city.

The sergeant takes me from one place to another all over town. Nobody has any information about the convoy and nobody has any idea what to do with me. By now I feel exhausted and am at my wits' end. I have been without sleep for nearly 36 hours and in a high state of anxiety nor have I had any food since our aborted meal in Lyon. What will they do with me if we draw a blank? We return to headquarters. It is now late afternoon. There is some whispered consultation. Then I move off again with my sergeant. Where will he take me now? We make our way through the busy streets to the big fortress which dominates the harbour. We enter the gates and to my utter consternation I see the sign 'FRENCH FOREIGN LEGION' . . .

They are billeted in the fortress. And I am being taken to that famous or rather infamous military institution. My heart sinks. I feel I want to run away, but there is no chance. I cling to the hope that they are perhaps just trying to find a bed for me for the night. Surely, they can't just dump me there against my will. Or can they?

I am delivered to the guardroom. The sergeant hands me over to the officer in charge. He takes my name and sends me off to a room full of new recruits. I try to plead and protest, but it is no good. I am told firmly not to leave the room. Totally exhausted after a long and terrible day and in utter despair I drop on my hard bed. I have landed up among the mercenaries of the world. I have reached absolute rockbottom.

Next morning we are roused at 6 am. There is black coffee and two biscuits for breakfast. At 7 am we line up for the roll-call in the courtyard. I am detailed with some of the other recruits to sweep the courtyard and the gutters. Later in the day we shall be properly enrolled. There is talk that in a few days we shall be moved to North Africa for a tour of duty lasting 18 months. The actual enrolment is for five years. I am beside myself with despair. And there is not a soul anywhere whom I can implore for help. I am trapped. I feel as though I have been sentenced to five years' penal servitude.

There is a marvellous view from the fortress over the harbour and the sea on one side and over the whole city of Marseille on the other. But in my present mood I can hardly appreciate it. Having done the chores I stand at the fortress wall and look idly down on the comings and goings down below. There is a steep drop and right down at the bottom is a road running past the fortress towards the harbour. It is that road on which I was brought to the Legion the previous evening.

While I glance at the life outside in the early morning sunshine and wish I was there and not here I suddenly spot on the road down below what looks to me like the officer in charge of our convoy. I must be hallucinating. It must we wishful thinking. But it is not. I look again and to my utter amazement I see the whole convoy squatting by the side of the road. What on earth are they doing there? And sure enough, there among them is Henry. Am I dreaming? No, I am not mistaken. There they are, evidently waiting for something to happen. And here I am just separated by a wall and a drop unable to communicate with them. So near and yet so far. I am in a panic that they might move on before I have had a chance to draw their attention to me. I rush to the guardroom. I try to explain to them that the group from which I had been separated was just outside the fortress. Please could I make contact with them. But, of course, they could not care less. I am told very firmly that I am now a Legionaire and that any attempt to make contact with the world outside will be severely punished. What can I do? Will freedom elude me when it is almost on the doorstep?

I ignore orders and run back to the wall and manage to

attract Henry's attention. He must think that he is seeing a ghost. Surrepticiously, I indicate that my hands are tied and that I am detained here. I scribble a brief note to explain my predicament and screw it up and drop it down. I don't care anymore if I am caught. I must try everything to regain my freedom.

The next thing that happens is that the officer in charge of our convoy comes through our gate and walks up the road that leads to the courtyard. I make a bee-line for him. In my excitement I can hardly get my words out. There is so much at stake at this moment. I try to explain to him that I was taken here by mistake and that I belong to the group down below for which he is responsible. Fortunately he recognises me at once. He goes off to have a word with the officer on duty in the office. A few agonizing moments for me. Will he ask for my release? He comes back and indicates that I am free to go with him. A few moments later we pass through the heavy gates of the fortress and I rejoin the convoy. It is wonderful to see Henry again and the rest of the group. I can hardly believe that I am free again. I was in the French Foreign Legion for just over 12 hours. I am still in a state of shock, but the nightmare is over. Almost as soon as I rejoin the convoy we move on. I could so easily have missed it this time!

Forty-five years later I still marvel at this quite extraordinary deliverance. It was nothing short of a miracle. To this day I can still see the convoy right down at the bottom of the rugged fortress wall and I still wonder whether it was all true. I am reminded of Peter in the Acts of the Apostles being imprisoned by Herod. And in the night an angel comes and opens the prison doors and leads him out. My dramatic deliverance from the Legion after just over twelve hours seems like divine intervention. No human explanation makes sense.

I suppose there are some factors which offer a few clues. But they are like odd pieces of a jigsaw which taken together make the perfect fit. As I found out later the convoy had arrived early that morning, sometime after our arrival in Marseille. The officer in charge had not been given clear instructions how to disperse us (the different nationalities were to be released to their respective repatriation camps). They made their way from the station through the city. When they came to the harbour area and saw that the Legion was stationed in the fortress they stopped there while the officer went inside to use the telephone and receive further instructions. It was during these vital minutes that I happened to spot the convoy down below and then saw the officer call in at the Legion. But the timing was so uncanny. Why did the convoy come this way? Why did I look over the wall just when it mattered? Why did the officer need to make the phone call? Why did the Legion not stop me from leaving again? They were all different pieces of the jigsaw, but they just came together in this quite miraculous way. In this desperate situation all things worked together for good. And in the end after all human reasons have been taken into account the only valid explanation for me is still that God rescued me. That experience had a profound and cumulative effect on my life. I became much more aware of God's guidance. I began to discern more clearly God's hand in my life. I eventually gave my life to him and his service. It was undoubtedly a critical turning point.

That, I am afraid, was by no means the end of all my problems. As the story of the next few months will reveal there were many more setbacks and disappointments, but I think I was better able to cope with them because I now believed with a deeper conviction that God was with me.

Well, back to the group outside the fortress. With my heart beating I rejoin the others. Needless to say they are extremely puzzled as to what had happened to me and why of all places I suddenly emerge from the Foreign Legion. As we move on I briefly relate my adventures since missing the train at Lyon. I also take possession again of my few belongings. Henry, ever hopeful, has held on to them. All is well again. For the moment. The next pressing question is what will happen next. The Poles and other nationalities will be discharged to their repatriation camps around Marseille. But there will not be any camps of that nature for Germans and Austrians. Our officer will have a problem to know how to dispose of us. However, that problem is solved sooner that we had expected. On the way we notice a sign 'Office of Jewish Aid'. Perhaps they will help us if we present our case to them. We ask our officer if we may stop off there and make enquiries. He has no objections. In fact, he is probably very relieved to let us go. Where else could he take us?

We call at the Jewish Aid Committee. They listen sympathetically to our story, but as we are not 'proper' Jews they regret that they cannot help us. But they know of a group of people who might. There is apparently a 'Comite' that is associated to the FFI and the Resistance Movement who are made up of dissident Germans. It is called 'FREE GERMANY'. We don't know anything about them, but they are clearly an anti-Nazi organization. Anything is better than nothing. We agree that we would like to meet them. After all we have to find shelter somewhere. We are sent off to the Comite. We are given a warm welcome in German. They give us something to eat (I had not eaten anything since I had those two biscuits first thing in the morning at the Legion). They take us to a place right on the outskirts of the city. We come to a rather dilapidated old mansion which seems to be occupied by Russians who had also fled from the Germans. A part of this is reserved for 'Free Germany'.

Here we meet Oskar who now takes charge of us. He has also escaped from the Todt Organisation. He is a Communist. So is apparently the whole Comite. Oskar explains to us that the movement 'Free Germany' originated in Russia. When the German armies were defeated at Stalingrad General von Seidtlitz surrendered to the Russians. He became one of their prize prisoners. He was taken to Moscow and later headed up this anti-Nazi movement. There are now branches of it in liberated parts of Europe and this is one of them. Oskar explains to us that he will train us to fight for the downfall of the Hitler regime. And he wastes no time initiating us. In the evening, after our sparse supper, our indoctrination begins with quotations from Lenin, Stalin, Dimitroff. We realise very quickly where we have landed up. Having left behind one militant ideology we now find ourselves caught up in another, no less insiduous. But we really had no choice, we needed to find a refuge somewhere. That evening, after the traumatic events of the day we are too tired to care for the moment. We simply flop into bed. At least we have a roof over our heads for the moment. The Foreign Legion seems a lifetime away!

Next morning we take stock of our new surroundings. 'We'

now means Henry, the two Austrians, Leo and Walter, and myself. We are in part of a larger building which must have seen better days. It now serves as military barracks. It is sparse and austere and is furnished with the bare essentials. It has a spacious garden and looks out on the rocky mountains behind Marseille. After the events of the last couple of days which have left me drained it is wonderful to enjoy peace and tranquillity, at least for the moment.

We are not left in peace for long. Our new 'comrades' naturally want to probe whether our stories are genuine and that we are not German soldiers in disguise. They take us to the Jewish Committee who will look into our background. We are introduced to a very sympathetic and cultured elderly gentleman, Rudolf Leonhard. He reminds me a little of Richard Strauss. He is a writer, left Germany in 1933 and has lived underground here in the South of France during the war years. He talks with us for over two hours about our family history, our life in the Todt Organisation, about Germany under the Nazis. It does not seem like an interrogation, but it probably gives him a fairly good idea who we are. We feel that he listens to us and appreciates that we are in need of help. He can't tell us at all what is likely to happen to us. He will make a report to the High Command of the FFI and they will have to decide.

In the evening we return by tram to La Pauline, the barracks where we are staying. We have no identity papers. It is quite nerve racking to travel on public transport without a pass. The authorities are still quite jumpy about 'fifth column' infiltrators and there are frequent checks on trams and buses. If we were caught we would have no proof of identity. We feel rather vulnerable.

When we get back to our quarters Oskar holds forth again about the blessings of Communism. He waxes eloquent about the prospect of being dropped by parachute into Germany and work as secret agents. Having just escaped from the clutches of the Nazis this is not quite our objective! But we keep quiet and withhold our comments. Each day we receive our indoctrination which we find quite trying, but we are at their mercy. One day, however, Walter, one of the Austrians who looks like a Hitler Youth, can't keep his mouth shut and runs into trouble. He expresses his dislike of Communism and that upsets Oskar. If we are not careful they can turn us out into the street again and what then? There are also tensions between Henry and me on the one hand and the two Austrians on the other. They assert their Austrian identity and don't want to make common cause with us. When one is thrown together in a fairly confined space such tensions make life more difficult.

Day after day we hang around in the 'Kaserne Pauline' and kick our heels. One day Otto, the Berliner, turns up and joins us. He went off to look for work when we arrived in Marseille, but, of course, could not find any. He is very lucky that the Police did not pick him up and that he has found us again. One day about thirty Yugoslavs move into our quarters and practically take the place over. We quickly gather our few belongings together because they lay their hands on anything that they can find. We retreat to a smaller room where we are very much on top of each other.

A member of the Comite visits us and raises our expectations. But he goes off again and we don't see him again. Beyond that nothing happens and nobody seems to make any decisions about us. We are bored stiff with doing nothing. We just sit and chat all day. We have no money, no tobacco, nothing to read. The food is barely enough. It consists mainly of onions and tomatoes, not a very appetizing daily diet! We have no identity papers, no legal status. We are really only safe within the confines of the barracks. That is probably why the Comite keeps us there.

By now it is almost two months since we made our escape. We had certainly expected then that we would be free and safe and recognised as refugees. Our patience is wearing thin and yet, there is very little we can do about it. Somebody must turn up soon. And sure enough one morning Werner, the man from the Comite who called before, drops in and takes us into town, to the Casa D'Italia. In the pre-war days it was apparently the centre and school of the Italian community in Marseille. It has been standing empty for some time. Now several foreign groups have established their offices there. Now the 'Free Germany' Comite have also been given a space there. But it is still full of junk from its wartime use. We clear the room of German ammunition and school desks which are piled right up to the ceiling and make the place habitable. This outing is a

*Curacy at Kilburn*

*Mission at Kilburn 1954 with students from CMS Training College led by Douglas Sargent, later Bishop of Selby*

welcome change from our daily monotony and gives us something to do.

While we are working there we have the chance of meeting
one or two members of the Comite who drop in to view their
new premises. There is Robert, the Colonel, who wears the
officer's uniform of the FFI. He seems to be the boss here and
has been active in the Resistance Movement during the war.
Then we meet Paul, a well educated man, a lawyer by profession as we find out later. He is an ardent socialist and fled
from the Nazis like the rest to work underground in France.
And there is Marcel who comes from Berlin and has been a
captain in the Resistance. He is also in uniform. There are also
one or two women who are either their wives or partners. One
day while we are working there Marcel gives us 50 francs. In
value very little, but it is the first money we have earned and
we feel like princes! With these coins in our pockets Henry and
I decide to take the risk of going to the pictures. And what a
treat this outing is. Simply to sit in plush seats in the cinema
instead of the hard chairs back at the barracks. For a couple of
hours we feel quite civilised. At the back of our minds is that
nagging fear that somebody might stop us and ask for our
identity cards. In the newsreel they show the march past of
American troops in front of General de Gaulle at the Place de
la Concorde.

On Sunday 5th November the Office is officially opened. It is
the first full meeting of the Comite. Anti-Nazi Germans who
have been in hiding during the Occupation come from various
parts of the South. A delegate from Lyon gives a brief survey
of the activities of this illegal group under the German occupation. They have all lived a very precarious existence in the
'maquis', their lives in constant danger of being caught or
betrayed. Now at long last they are free and meet to consider
the next move. The objectives of the Comite are being debated.
A provisional Council of the Comite is elected with Leonhard
(who interviewed us) as Chairman. The official status of the
Comite in relation to the FFI is not yet clear. They have been
tolerated, but are not formally recognised. After the meeting
which we are allowed to attend we have a brief word with
Leonhard about our future. He says that he has spoken on our
behalf to the High Command of the FFI, but has not heard

anything from them about our legitimisation. Although it is of vital importance to us the French authorities have probably more important and urgent matters to think about in these early days after the liberation.

We sit around again for some days and get more and more exasperated with Oskar's attempts to turn us into Communists. There is another angry confrontation between him and Walter. This time Leo, the other Austrian, joins in as well. We keep quiet because we fear that the Comite will throw us out if we don't conform. After all, we are a liability to them which could be an embarrassment for them. Henry and I are a little worried. However, after a few days there is another job for us. The Comite has found a derelict restaurant which might be useful as a canteen. But it needs to be thoroughly cleaned. It is filthy and neglected. First we have to clear out all the rubbish and then decorate it from top to bottom. It is a terrible job and we get covered in dust. We have no change of clothes except what we wear. But at least it keeps us occupied for a few days.

We are now also experiencing another discomfort. The winter is setting in and the weather is noticeably turning colder. There is no heating in the Kaserne nor in the restaurant where we are working. Our rather flimsy clothes were alright during the milder weather, but they are quite inadequate for the winter. So we shiver most of the time and wish we could get hold of some warmer clothes. But we have no money to buy anything and in any case there are as yet few clothes in the shops. One day I am called to the Comite. They offer me a job as typist, both in German and French. The pay is very poor, but it will give me some pocket money and at least I will have a regular job for the time being. It is much better to be occupied than to sit around in the Kaserne. It also gives me the opportunity of seeing more of the Comite members. Perhaps my presence will remind them that we are still without identity papers. My immediate boss is Paul. He runs the office and drafts reports and minutes and memoranda. He dictates letters and reports to me. I have an old typewriter which has seen better days. To my great surprise I find that I can manage dictation and typing quite well, even though I have to take everything down in long hand. It also helps to improve my

French. At long last things are looking up and life is a little more interesting. We prepare for a big conference in December. Some days I am really quite busy. For this I receive the princely sum of 330 francs. A pittance really, but suddenly I feel quite rich!

Robert, the Colonel, who heads up the Comite, is quite amazed when I tell him that we still have no papers. But they have to be quite circumspect themselves. The Comite is not yet formally recognised by the French authorities. As it originated in Russia and its ideology is Communist it is suspect in the eyes of the French. I understand that the executive members of the Comite will have a meeting with General Schmidt, the Commander-in-Chief of the French Army in Marseille about the official recognition. If it receives legal status it will probably make it easier for us to obtain the necessary papers. Herr Leonhard also assures me again that he will raise our case with the municipal authorities at the next opportunity. But we never know whether they are just politely putting off a decision about us.

In the meantime I go backwards and forwards on the buses and trams each day and am relieved every time I get home safely. Paul, my immediate boss, who feels responsible for me consults other members of the Comite and thinks that they may be able to obtain faked papers for us which show that we have worked in the Maquis (the Resistance Movement). This lack of identity proves a problem for poor Henry. One day he goes down with a high temperature. Next morning he shakes like a leaf and the two Austrians take him to the nearest hospital. To begin with it looks like acute tonsilitis. But, in fact, it is diphtheria and he is moved to an isolation hospital. Henry has to pretend that he is a Yugoslav who has lost his papers. We hope they won't find out who he is and hand him over to the police.

One evening after a hard day's work at the office taking dictation and typing long reports Paul, my boss, invites me back to his home. This is the first time since leaving home in April that I am inside a nice and comfortable and adequately furnished apartment. It takes some getting used to. I have almost forgotten how to behave in a civilised manner and to sit at a table that has been laid for dinner. There is even real coffee at the end of the meal to round it off. That must have come from the black market. Afterwards there is good and relaxed conversation. Just for one evening I can forget my problems and the uncertainties about the future.

A few evenings later we are forcefully reminded of the opposite, the harsh realities of life although the war is over (at least down here). A number of Yugoslavs and Czechs arrive at the barracks from a PoW Camp near St Tropez where they had been held until now. We listen to their terrible stories – one loaf of bread per day for six, twice a day some watery soup. No soap, no proper sanitary facilities. Apparently, many have died of hunger. That must be the same for many other prisoners. It could have been our lot. We have cause to grumble in our rather primitive surroundings and monotonous food, but by comparison we are still very much better off than many others.

We now have a lady typist in the office who is much better qualified than I am. She is French, Madame Michael. She sympathises with my plight and offers her help in obtaining the necessary papers for me. She will go with me to the Prefecture. The Comite give me a piece of paper to certify that I am a member and that I work for them. At long last there is a little bit of progress. I have to fill in the formal 'demande' (application) for the Prefecture. In fear and trembling I go with Madame to see the Chef de Service des Etrangers. I wonder how he will react to my application. To my great relief the interview does not take any time. He is very pleasant and issues a certificate on the spot valid for two months. It probably helped having a French citizen to introduce me. I still have to go to the Police and be interrogated by them. But for the moment I am safe. I have a legal piece of paper on me and I can travel on public transport without worrying whether I am going to be stopped. It also means that at long last I can go to the Ration Bureau and obtain a ration card – for bread, for other essential food, for tobacco. I feel no longer like an outcast who has to keep out of sight, but a little more like a human being.

Armed with this paper I make another visit to the British Consulate which is now manned by British officials. But even they are not very helpful. They regret that they cannot facilitate any contact with my father. Nor can they suggest any suitable work for me. Although I have some work at the Comite I am not very comfortable in an atmosphere which is dominated by Communism. I would gladly find something a little more congenial. But where to look? For the time being I have to carry on at the Comite. There is even an incentive that my wages might be increased to 1,000 francs a month. And possibly accommodation. That would be wonderful. I begin to feel less and less secure at the Kaserne. Recently we were woken up several nights running when some of our Yugoslav neighbours and others (including our carefree Berliner) came back completely drunk and making a frightful noise.

In the office we work right up to the last minute to get all the paperwork out for the Conference. It opens on Saturday with a large number of delegates. Suddenly, in the middle of the opening session, Henry appears, looking thin and pale. He has been in three hospitals. He says that he has been given very good treatment, and also good food. He managed to keep up the pretence that he was a Yugoslav. It is good to see him back again. On the Sunday the Conference goes on all day with talks and discussion on the future of the movement and its role both in France and in Germany. We tuck into a very good lunch which is served to all the delegates. More discussion and election of officers in the afternoon. The Conference ends with Leonhard, the Chairman, reading some of his poetry which reflects on the German occupation and the underground movement. How did they survive the long years of the occupation? They must have had many anxious moments when their lives were in danger.

With my piece of paper I can go at long last to the Food Bureau and claim my ration cards. Next I queue alongside the local people and claim the small ration to which I am entitled. It is really quite an event to buy something as basic as bread. And it makes a welcome change from the monotonous diet of tomatoes and onions.

As I was told at my visit to the Prefecture I still have to be investigated by the Police. The story that the Comite persuaded me to produce and that I put in my 'demande' is that I emigrated to France in 1939, that I have been in the underground movement during the occupation and that I have lost my papers which can prove this. I would certainly not pass if the authorities discovered that I had escaped from the Todt Organisation though we were victims of the Nazis. I am sure the Comite were right in persuading me to make up this story, but I feel very uneasy about it. I fear that one day the true story will be discovered and then I shall be in deep trouble. I shall refer to it again later because for the rest of my time in France I worry about it. I now go to the Police in some trepidation armed with another paper from the Comite to say that I have been in the Resistance. The official takes down my particulars. We talk about the defeat of Germany and about the Comite (by now I am fairly fluent in French). After half an hour we part with a friendly handshake. There seems to be no problem. I feel greatly relieved that the interview is over. It was hardly an interrogation. A few days later I receive my formal identity card from the FFI which I still possess. To all intents and purposes I am now fully legitimised. While I was without any papers I was really stuck with the Comite. I was relatively safe at the Kaserne and in the office. The daily journey on public transport was risky. Now with these precious identity papers I feel quite secure to move around Marseille. And now I can think of making a move if I can find work elsewhere.

Henry and the two Austrians have already put out feelers to the Americans in search of some work. I go and see a Mr Oppenheimer at the American Employment Bureau. I want to find out what my chances are of getting a job with them. I have come to the conclusion that in the long run there is no future for me working for the Comite. I shall be stuck at the typewriter day after day writing reports. I cannot see what purpose they serve. 'Free Germany' seems to be a freak movement made up of radical left-wing emigres and refugees who nourish the hope of running a future Germany, but here in Marseille they are out on a limb. If it were not for the fact that some of their members had senior positions in the Resistance they would probably be prohibited. Their Communist philosophy does not appeal to me. Sooner or later I need to get out. I also find it difficult to manage on 1,000 francs a month, especially as inflation is pushing prices up. However, there is no opening with the Americans at the moment, but Mr Oppenheimer (who is fluent in German and French) assures me that something will turn up before long. He encourages me to try again.

When I call at his office two days later I am offered a job as 'checker' at the port. It is well paid. It means checking supplies for the troops which are being unloaded at the harbour. I report the following night with two Spaniards and two Frenchmen. We are taken down to the harbour and given some instructions about our work. But, alas, after that first night I have to say 'no' to it. It is shiftwork, 12 hours day or night, and no day off. It is out in the open in the middle of winter. I have no warm clothes and I am frozen stiff that first night. I can't cope in those conditions.

I go back to the Comite and speak to Paul, my boss. I explain to him that I have been looking for a better paid job as I can't manage on their pay. He has some sympathy and the result is that he doubles my wages to 2,000 francs (of which 1,400 goes on food). He also still hopes to find me some digs and warmer clothes. I badly need at least a pullover to keep me warm. The weather is getting much colder. There is practically no heating anywhere. In my diary there are frequent references to shivering both in the barracks and in the office. Even sleeping is difficult because we don't have enough blankets. My shoes are disintegrating and let the rain in. I sit in the office all day with frozen feet. It is surprising that I don't catch pneumonia.

My companions are on the move now. Leo has found a room for the two Austrians. We are not sorry that they are leaving us. Henry is offered a job as driver with the Americans and starts the following day. He is driving a Jeep and can use it for private runs as well. He is also looking out for a room. Naturally, that makes me restless, too. I feel somehow left behind. If only a suitable job turned up with the Americans! I have to be patient and hope that my turn will come.

# 6

# First Contacts with England

THE thought of eventually making my way to England is never far from my mind. At this time just before Christmas 1944 my diary records a significant move in that direction. Significant, for it eventually leads to my goal – the reunion with my father. The British Consulate, quite understandably, was not interested in me when I called. I had no personal recommendation for an introduction. And in my shabby clothes and dilapidated shoes I probably looked more like a tramp. But I remembered from our correspondence with my father just before the outbreak of war that the Bishop of Chichester, Dr George Bell, had taken some interest in my father and certainly knew him. Postal communications with England are just beginning to be resumed. So I decide to sit down and compose a letter to 'The Bishop of Chichester, Chichester, England'. Whether this address will reach him and whether he will take any notice of my letter is another matter. But it is worth trying. Here is the letter I wrote. I found it only recently among my father's papers. My English then was still very poor and I think somebody helped me whose knowledge of English was just a little better!

> Dear Sir,
> I am Juergen Simonson, the son of Reverend Werner Simonson who emigrated to England in 1939 and met you in London. You have been kind enough to take care of him so that he got a free study at the Cheshunt College in Cambridge. Since 1942 he is employed at a Christ Church in London. That is all I know about him That is why I ask if you know the residence of my father. Perhaps you could inform him that you got this letter and tell him that I am waiting for a cablegram from him. When the Germans left France in September 1944 I escaped of them and since the middle of October 1944 I am working with the Anti-Nazi Movement 'Free Germany' at Marseille. You understand, dear Sir, that I would like to see my father after six years' separation and I should be much obliged to you if you could find a way to do something for me, perhaps through the British

Consulate here – 1 rue d'Arcole, Marseille. I thank you very much in advance and remain, dear Sir,

Yours faithfully

Juergen Simonson

This letter actually reached the Bishop a month later. But that is jumping ahead and I shall come back to it later.

I had dreaded the approach of Christmas as a refugee in a foreign land and feared that it would be very lonely and spartan and dreary. In fact, it turned out to be much brighter than I had anticipated. To my great surprise I am invited to the home of one of the senior members of the Comite, together with several other German emigres. Hans, our host, talks about his opposition to the Nazis as a Communist, his time in a concentration camp, and then his underground activities here in the South of France. We are treated to a real Christmas dinner which is amazing in these times of rationing – meat and wine and even a proper German 'Stollen'! We can hardly believe our eyes, certainly food that I had not seen for many months. And that it not the end of Christmas night. When we leave our host I am invited to join some of the others in a restaurant which the Comite patronise. And there is yet more food. We celebrate till the early hours of the morning. Actually, we have no choice but to stay there till 6 am when the first tram will take us back to the Kaserne. Then I crash out and wake up sometime during the afternoon.

It is quite remarkable that we can enjoy proper Christmas fare. There is a note in my diary to make the point that prior to Christmas only small amounts of coffee and noodles are available on the ration books. For Christmas there is an extra allocation of meat, oil – and for the first time – cheese. However, the French grumble about this meagre concession and blame poor administration.

And so the eventful year 1944 draws to a close. 'The most difficult year of my life,' I write in my diary, 'it brought separation from home, the escape from the Nazis, and a very precarious and unpredictable life in exile. I have to stand on my own feet, probably the best way to prepare me for the future. As I look ahead to the New Year it looks very gloomy indeed, with Germany heading for the abyss. It is about to face the most horrific chaos. I go to bed tonight with an unfaltering confidence in God's grace which in spite of all troubles has so clearly blessed me so far.' My thoughts are with my parents in Germany, in England, and my ardent prayer is that the New Year will bring a safe reunion. All the signs are that 1945 will see at long last the end of the war. The New Year begins with a cold spell, with ice and frost, even down here in the South of France. There is still no heating anywhere and I feel like a block of ice. The Comite give me two pairs of woollen American socks – in these circumstances a royal gift.

All these discomforts are soon forgotten when on the evening of 5th January I receive a telegram from the Marchant-Hacots in Paris (who sheltered us in the Chapelotte and with whom I had kept in touch): 'Received today cable from your father. We have cabled reply that you are well. Letter follows.' I am absolutely over the moon. This is the moment I have been waiting for ever since we escaped. At long last the first contact with my father is made. He knows that I am alive and that I am in Marseille. My mind is buzzing with all kinds of heady expectations. I could not wish for a more propitious start to the New Year. Surely, sometime during this year I should see my father again.

A few days later I hear from the Marchant-Hacots with my father's address – 52 Walham Grove, London SW6. I had written to him from Gray a few days after our escape telling him what had happened to us and giving him the Marchant-Hacots' address in Paris. That note was sent to the British Red Cross, the only address I knew. He must have received that note after some delay and responded to it by writing to my friends in Paris. Apparently, he had also cabled some money. I rush straightaway to the Post Office to find out if there is a telegram and the money, but no luck yet. Even cables still take some time. In turn, I send off a cable to him: 'Received your cable to Paris. Hope for early reunion with you. Overjoyed . . .' Things are beginning to happen, but how long it will take to get all the necessary papers is anybody's guess.

Henry is now working for the Americans. Indirectly, I benefit from it. He can pick up food in the US Army canteen where he eats and share it with me. It is a treat to have a little more variety. He also gives me occasionally lifts in his Jeep. It gives us an elated sense of freedom to move around Marseille without feeling inhibited by fears of being apprehended as irregular aliens.

For the first time there is an entry in the diary about a Jean Meyerowitz, a German Jew and a professional musician. I have come across him at the Comite and he takes an interest in me. He gives concerts in Marseille and when I tell him of my (genuine) interest in music he offers me a complimentary ticket for one of his piano recitals. His modern music is not quite my taste, but that does not matter. Again, as when we went to the Cinema, it is a treat to sit in a good seat in the Concert Hall and imbibe some culture. We shall hear more of the Meyerowitzs.

There is another cable from my father in which he says that the Bishop of Chichester has applied for a permit for me. The Bishop wrote to him on 19th January:

> You will be delighted to see a copy of a letter from your son to me dated 23rd December. It is good news. I have written today to Sir Alexander Maxwell (Under-Secretary at the Home Office) sending him a copy of your son's letter; and I have also written to Pastor Boegner (head of the Protestant Church in France).

At the end of January I receive the first letter from my father. I write back to him:

> You can't imagine my great joy when I actually saw your writing after such a long time. With two friends I have celebrated this event with two aperitifs! I am so happy that you are well and that your work gives you much strength. Unfortunately, I have not yet received the money that you sent me. I expect it any day.

But that joy is tinged with anxiety. I find myself in a great conflict of loyalties. Having at long last got in touch with my father I am now determined to get to England and be reunited with him and begin a new life there. However, working in a German anti-Nazi organization I am told daily that a defeated and demoralised Germany needs now our single-minded help. This seems a perfectly plausible argument. The members of the Comite assume that those who work for them would consider it their duty to go back to Germany and work for the reconstruction of the country as soon as this is practicable. I find it a tantalising problem. I put this to my father in the same letter as above:

> As far as I am concerned, I am well. I have some work. But otherwise I am not happy because I have a problem. If you can't bring me over to England soon I shall have to go with our members to fight in Germany against the Nazi regime. I love my country, but you will understand that I am not very anxious to go with them. Because just at the moment when at long last I have made contact with you I don't want to risk my life in the final struggle of Germany, Also these people on the Comite don't like the idea that I want to see you again. They are politically minded and have no time for family. They are very left-wing. My sympathies are with England. I expect that it is bound to take some time for you to bring me over. I am terribly afraid that in the meantime I shall have to go with the Comite and I shall not see you. It is a difficult problem and I don't now what to do. There is nobody I can talk to because they just would not understand. I have to wait and see. God has guided me till now and I am sure that he will direct the way that is best for me.

This matter comes to a head one day when I am called in to the Colonel, the head of the Comite. He asks me the leading question: Would I be prepared to go to Germany as a 'partisan' to fight for the liberation of the country. I am in a real state. What can I possibly say? They would expect an unambiguous 'yes' from me. In their minds there is no question that their followers would want to liberate their country. But I know that if one was dropped over Germany the chances of being caught and killed were great. Just at this moment the opportunity of beginning a new life in England is opening up for me and I am denied that hope if I am sent to Germany instead. I ask for time to consider. This, of course, does not go down well at all. The members of the Comite show their disappointment and imply that I am a coward. What am I to do? My letter to my father must have been written just after this interview had taken place.

After the weekend I go back to the Colonel and very reluctantly agree that I am prepared to go. I can't delay my response because I know that it is bound to take weeks to obtain my papers to go to England. I would need to get out of the clutches of the Comite now and that is not possible. My reply and its implications leave me in a very worried and unsettled state.

From now I hear fairly regularly from my father. He is at a Church in Fulham in South London. He tells me that via our friends in Switzerland he has heard that my mother is well. That is a great relief to me. Since my escape I had, of course, no news from her and I was afraid all the time that the Nazis might take some reprisals against her. But I wonder anxiously what will happen to her with the Russians steadily advancing towards East Germany. I mention again to my father my fear of having to go back to Germany. I ask him whether he could possibly visit me in Marseille so that at least we could meet again. Looking back on that suggestion now I realise that I must have been very naive to think that travelling to France would have been possible.

One day when I call again at the Bank the money that my father has sent has arrived. I promptly go to the shoe repairer and acquire a second-hand pair of shoes. I feel as though I am walking on air after the last and only pair had nearly disintegrated.

One day Jean Meyerowitz whom I mentioned earlier invites me to his home where I meet his charming girlfriend, Marguerite Fricker, and two of his friends. One is a well-known Marseille lawyer, the other a flautist, Jean-Pierre Rampal. He later becomes one of the leading international flautists and can still be heard today. It is a most enjoyable evening. The lawyer talks to me at great length and is very interested to hear of my experiences which I later have to relate to the whole company. After a very good meal Meyerowitz and Rampal play together – Haydn, Reinecke and some compositions by Meyerowitz himself. The evening in my present unsettled state is a great tonic. When Meyerowitz sees me off at the tram stop I share my fears with him. He understands, but assures me that as a member of the Comite he has some say in their decisions. He tells me not to worry.

I tell my father about this wonderful evening. I also respond to a question which he must have raised in one of his first letters. What would I like to do if I came over to England? He would then begin to put out some feelers for me:

About the study of Theology I have not yet quite made up my
mind. There was a time when I was not very keen on the idea.
But after the last few months when I have received so many
blessings from God I am again strengthened in my faith in God.
For a long time I have been very interested in music and I am
still very keen on it. But I think it is too expensive to study it
and I am probably too old for it. I don't know what to do. I
think I could probably find much satisfaction and joy in theology. Should the Bishop of Chichester give me his backing this
might be the best thing for me to do. We need to talk more
about this, but it is important now that you should know my
present inclinations.

It is interesting to see that by this time my mind was moving in
the direction of theological training. Probably I saw it more as
an academic subject and not yet as a ministry of Word and
Sacrament. But quite clearly God was at work in me and
leading me on to more profound spiritual experiences of
Himself.

I am still plodding on at the Comite, but with less and less
motivation. Henry turns up from time to time in his Jeep and
takes me out for lunch. The accommodation at the cold and
spartan Kaserne in the middle of winter is very uncomfortable.
I long to get away from there. And then lo and behold, almost
overnight everything changes for the better.

# 7

# A New Address and
# a New Job

IT is now the early part of February. Suddenly, several things
happen which turn out to be a real turning point in my
circumstances. One morning the office of the Comite is closed
down. Unfortunately my diary does not mention the reason
for it. I think we were just told not to come in and were not
told why. My guess is that the Comite was suspect in the eyes
of the French authorities because of its Communist leanings
and its connection with Russia. It means that I am suddenly
out of work, but it also means that at long last my involvement
in the 'Free Germany' Movement is at an end. It seems
providential.

I suppose Meyerowitz, as a member of the Comite, must
have heard that I am at a loose end. He contacts me and offers
me a spare room in his house. I can't wish for anything better
and am deeply touched by his kindness. At long last I can get
out of the dingy conditions at the barracks and leave my two
companions with whom I have shared the room. They were
quite pleasant, but I have very little in common with them and
I have no regrets parting with them. One of my room mates at
the Kaserne warns me that I shall regret the move. What I
think he means is that the Comite will no longer have any hold
on me. They are losing one of their recruits for the liberation
of Germany.

Looking back on that period now – some 4–5 months – I
must be thankful that I was provided with a roof over my
head and that I had some work and pay to keep body and soul
together. I met some interesting people whose courage during
the long years 'underground' I greatly admired. But ideologi-
cally I was never at home in that atmosphere. I still remember
that first night when we were at once indoctrinated with
Communist slogans. Now after that trying time I can turn my
back on it and look forward to what can only be a better and

much more congenial environment for me. I never see anything again of my bosses at the Comite – Paul and Marcel and Robert, the Colonel, and their camp followers. I have often wondered what became of them all. I wonder whether they did return to Germany. I don't think that dramatic parachute drop to liberate the country ever took place and I need not have worried about my part in it. I doubt whether the French army would have recruited them for such an engagement. At any rate, it was one anxiety which I could now put behind me. One good move is followed by another. Being out of work I call again at the American Employment Bureau. They give me an English test and to my great surprise they are satisfied with my knowledge. I think they must have given me the benefit of the doubt. It is quite amazing that I scrape through because my English is still very poor. Some of the English that I was taught at school must have sunk in. Anyway, the result of this test is that I am offered a clerical job in their Transportation Office. This is situated in the building of the Colonial Museum at the Rond Point opposite Henry's car pool. It is surrounded by large public gardens, very pleasant. I earn 4,500 francs (twice as much as before) and there are official office hours. It is all very civilised. With these two moves, a new home and a new job, life becomes much more bearable.

The Meyerowitzs' house is on the outskirts of Marseille right by the sea. I have a pleasant room and enjoy some privacy, for the first time since leaving home. It is such a change from our bare existence in the Kaserne. I am welcomed and treated as a member of the family. Once again I feel that God has intervened, first through the initial meeting with Meyerowitz and then by providing me with such a comfortable place.

I recall a rather amusing anecdote, amusing now as I look back on it, but rather disillusioning for me at the time. I have mentioned the charming and good-looking Maitre whom I had met socially at the Meyerowitzs and who had taken such a keen interest in my situation. I was quite impressed with his solicitude and must have mentioned it to my mates before I moved. Their response was to warn me that this man was probably gay. I was outraged that this could even cross their minds. How ridiculous! Such a delightful and cultured person, and a senior member of his profession. This was quite out of the question. I must admit that in those days I was still very innocent. I knew very little about homosexuals and probably had never come across any. How great was my shock a few days later when I moved to the Meyerowitzs and was going to meet the Maitre again. Jean took me aside and gently pointed out to me that this friend whom he greatly respected was a homosexual and had a liking for younger people. He recommended that I should not yield too much to his charms. Just as well I was told! I still remember him well and can see now what I would not have perceived then.

The letter that I had sent to the Bishop of Chichester must have reached him at last. I am greatly cheered when I receive a telegram from him which says: 'Letter received and forwarded to your father who is well. We are making efforts to bring you to England, but some delay unavoidable.' The prospect of going to England instead of being dropped over Germany becomes more of a reality.

In the middle of these new promising developments in my life comes the shattering news of the bombing of Dresden on St Valentine's Day. Whereas most other German cities had been bombed for some strange reason not a single bomb had fallen on Dresden. There were rumours that the Allies were trying to preserve one city as the administrative centre of Germany after the war or that it was spared because of its cultural treasures. Dresden was called the 'Florence of the Elbe' and had been a popular tourist centre before the war. It had a famous Opera and an equally famous Picture Gallery. And now it had been totally devastated in 24 hours of American and British air-raids. The papers likened its fate to that of Hiroshima. The number of casualties will never be known. The town was choked with refugees from the East fleeing from the Russians. They were in emergency accommodation in halls and schools and churches. It is reckoned that between 35,000 and 100,000 people perished in the firestorm that engulfed the city. (My mother's personal account of that night is on page 24).

Much has been written about these raids. They were meant to destabilise the Nazi resistance and facilitate the Russian advance into Germany. They were of no direct military value (there were no military targets in Dresden), but hit mainly the civilian population and reduced many precious historic sites to rubble. There are pictures of burnt corpses piled high in the Altmarkt in the centre of Dresden because the emergency services could not find enough burial places for such numbers.

For me the news is a devastating blow. Partly because I love the city and am still emotionally attached to it. But much more because I wonder whether my mother is still alive, and if she is, what will have happened to her. Our home is not far from the centre and quite close to the main railway station. It could hardly have escaped the bombing. And what makes it worse is that there is no way to make enquiries about her. I write to my father:

> I am full of sadness and great fear about Leonie. All my thoughts are with her and with you. I don't hold out much hope for her, and if I still have a slender hope it is because I trust in God. He has protected us three until now. These are terrible days for her and I am so sad that I am far from her.

The work in the American office is very slack. In fact, I am surprised that they gave me a job because there is not enough to do. The office is well heated, the days of shivering at the Comite are over.

> My boss is very kind and I also earn more money. I work there from 8 o'clock in the morning till 5.30 in the evening which is very convenient. The other advantage is that I now have to speak English. I want to learn it as quickly as possible.

At lunchtime I usually meet Henry, in the evenings I enjoy the congenial company of M. Meyerowitz and Mlle Fricker. My father seems to pull out all the stops for me. I hear from a British Army Chaplain, John Millar-Craig who sends me some second-hand clothing which I badly need. I also gather that the Chaplain of the British Embassy in Paris, Williams-Ashman, is trying to use his influence on my behalf at the British Consulate there. I feel much more supported about the future. One evening the Maitre invites me to a meal at a black market restaurant. The delicious meal, the best I have had for years, comes to 560 francs. I am lost for words! That would keep me for a week. Fortunately, I don't have to pay for it, I can just enjoy the treat. After the meal we go to his well appointed apartment. I am a little apprehensive after Meyerowitz's warning, but the evening passes off very pleasantly. He tries to persuade me to stay for the night, but being well aware of the hazard I insist that I must get back. He sends me off with a warm pullover. On the Sunday Meyerowitz and I go for a lovely stroll along the sea. Then some friends come for lunch, including Jean-Pierre Rampal. In the evening I listen their music-making – Frederick the Great, Bach, Mozart. Mlle Fricker sings some lovely songs by Cornelius. A wonderful evening.

I call again at the British Consulate where at first I am given a cool reception. But when I produce the Bishop's telegram and other correspondence they begin to show more interest. Eventually I am seen by the First Secretary. I tell him my story and my connections with England whereupon he gives me an application form for a visa which I have to complete and which will be forwarded to Paris. This is another important step. I shall need an exit permit from the French authorities. I am a little worried how they will view my application and whether they will let me go. I shall have to stick to the story which the Comite made up for me, but I feel uneasy about it.

I write to my father about this visit:

> The Secretary asked me what I was intending to do in England. I said that I would gladly do some war service or study theology. He gave me two questionnaires which I have to fill in. They will ask the Passport Office in Paris to issue a Passport to England. He could not say if the Passport would be granted. But I think it is a good sign that they will at least try to obtain a Visa for me.
>
> I keep thinking of the moment when I shall arrive at one of the Railway Stations in London and meet you on the platform and we are happy together after 6 years of separation. Today I think of 7th March six years ago when we were on the platform in Dresden and saw you off. It was one of the saddest moments of my life. Then I was still a child, now I am a young man. I am not angry against God about these years. On the contrary, I am very thankful to him because I have learnt so much during this time which otherwise I would never have known.

John Millar-Craig, the British Army Chaplain whom I mention earlier unexpectedly finds himself posted to Marseille and one day he turns up out of the blue. He and my father were fellow students in Cambridge. He has seen my father fairly recently and can give me first-hand news about him. I gather from him that my father works in a large Anglican parish in South London and is Assistant (Curate) to the Vicar. He lives in digs and is well looked after. John is a delightful person, caring and anxious to help. I immediately take to him. My first direct contact with England. We have a long talk. The next day he accompanies me to the British Consulate to submit my completed application. His presence there makes all the difference. We see the Vice-Consul who is very friendly and forthcoming. My application will now go via Paris to London. He warns me that at the moment the British authorities do not admit foreigners into the country. He hopes, however, that they might make an exception in this case.

Among his duties John has pastoral responsibility for German PoW Camps around Marseille. He wonders whether I might like to help him with one or two of the services which he has to take in the camps. He has a smattering of German, but obviously it would be very helpful to have somebody there who is fluent. Would I like to preach? Here is a challenge!

The next step towards my attempts to go to England is to obtain the necessary exit papers from the French authorities. Meyerowitz offers to go with me to the Prefecture to make enquiries about it. We see the Secretary of the Section for Foreigners. Meyerowitz tells him my story. They will probably extend my certificate for my stay in France. But to obtain an Exit Visa is a different matter. The application would have to go to the highest military authorities and it is doubtful whether they would give me permission to leave the country. They are (rightly) hypersensitive after the very recent Occupation and are still in the process of bringing war criminals to justice. It might well mean that before long I would get an Entry Visa into Britain, but cannot leave France. At least not for the time being. That is not such good news.

One evening John Millar-Craig takes me out to dinner at the British Officers' Club. I would have laughed in disbelief if somebody had predicted this a few weeks earlier. For the first time I am in a proper British environment. I note in my diary that I confide in John (and perhaps for the first time admit to myself) that I want to study theology when I settle in England.

This has been a gradual subconscious process arising out of the hard and at times remarkable experiences of the last few months. In all the ups and downs – and there have been so many – I have been very much aware of God's guidance and protection.

There have been many occasions when things could have turned out very differently and could have gone badly wrong. But time and again I have felt that God was with me. Now I am slowly beginning to realise that it may mean on my part to offer my life to God in whatever way he may want to use me. At present this is more an intellectual and individualistic response. As yet I don't go to Church. I have very little opportunity in Marseille to do so. To be a member of that corporate body is not yet part of my spiritual experience. But in an unexpected way that opportunity now presents itself.

As I mention above John asks me to assist him with his services among German prisoners of war. That is a tall order. I have never taken part in a religious service other than sit in the congregation. I have never yet spoken in public. I have no experience of preaching. Where do I begin? I feel very apprehensive and ill-equipped. I recall the verse that my Pastor in Dresden gave me at my Confirmation in 1939 'Lord, to whom shall I go? You have the words of eternal life' (John 6.68). At the time I realised that he had found just the right word for me. It fitted my condition perfectly. My future was quite uncertain and became even more unpredictable in the years that followed. I did not know where I was going. I was completely in the dark, especially when I was called up for forced labour. That verse has remained my spiritual motto ever since. While it means a great deal to me personally I also feel that it would be quite appropriate to these prisoners in similar circumstances.

On Good Friday 1945 John picks me up in his Jeep and drives me to one of the large German PoW Camps some way out of Marseille. I am introduced to a schoolteacher who seems to act as a kind of pastor in the camp and has taken some of the services himself. We gather in one of the huts, about 100 men crowded together. They are standing throughout, there is no room to sit. These men have been defeated.

They are demoralised. They probably have no news of their families at home. They are completely in the dark about their future and that of their country. They have come to this service because they are in desperate need of help and hope and encouragement. They need God's comfort. As I look into their sad faces on that Good Friday I realise what a responsibility it is to speak to them when I am a complete novice myself. I remember that I suffer from what one would call 'stage fright' before the service (after a sleepless night), I feel so utterly inadequate to address this enormous need that confronts me in that prison hut.

I begin my address with a reference to a book which had made a deep impression on me and which had been widely read in Germany before I left. It was by one of their leading writers, Ernst Wiechert, and was called *Das einfache Leben* (The Simple Life). It was, in fact, anything but simple. I seem to remember that the hero of the book had lost everything. He retreats to an island off the German coast and tries to rebuild his life from scratch. It was a prophetic book anticipating what was going to happen to Germany. The key phrase which stands out in my mind is 'we must all begin again'. It was, I think, a coded message to the readers implying the collapse of the Nazi regime.

Starting from that phrase I remind this congregation that, yes, they have lost everything, they don't know where they go, where to turn, but God has the words of life, not of death. The Christian message offers the hope of a new beginning. On that Good Friday I try to relate their condition to the death and resurrection of Jesus Christ who says 'Behold, I make all things new'.

I have no idea what that first sermon is like, whether I am able to communicate what I want to convey, whether it meets their need. But they listen. You can see that they are eager to pick up anything that offers them some kind of assurance and faith. However, the significance of the sermon for *me* is the effect that it has on my life in the long run.

I quote from my diary: 'In preaching for the first time I feel that this calling would give me a sense of deep satisfaction and fulfilment . . . I feel very happy that for the first time I am able to serve God in this way'. I write at the end of the day that it will probably be one of the decisive days of my life. And in retrospect this is no exaggeration. It was on that Good Friday 1945 that I believe I received a call from God. I try to express my feelings to my father:

> I know now that I shall become a pastor and that it will be a good job for me (it is one of my first letters in English previously I had written in French). I am still under the impression of that day. But I am sorry that I cannot describe all my feelings by letter. I cannot find words. You can imagine that I was a little anxious before the service. But I can say that all was well. I spoke my sermon before nearly a hundred men who listened to my words with a sincere composure. They were old and young men and I had the feeling that they really needed to listen to God's Word. Never, in the last years, have I observed such a positive attitude to God. I was very astonished because I had not believed to find such men. I was surprised when I heard that nearly all men wanted to take afterwards the Holy Communion. We were sorry we could not give it. It was too late and my friend had only brought bread and wine for ten men. I preached 25 minutes, we prayed together and we sang, too. My English friend gave the blessing, I could not preach by heart, you will understand, because I have not yet enough experience. I thought the whole time if only you could be present at the service. Of course, I shall keep my sermon and show it to you later. Very, very happy I went back to Marseille with my friend.

After the service I talk for a short time to several of the prisoners and am impressed with their general outlook. It gives me hope for the Germany of the future. Returning home that evening I drop into bed dead tired after the nervous strain of the day, but also very thankful to have had this profound spiritual experience.

We are now at the end of March and every news item reports fresh advances of the allied armies into Germany. The final offensive for the defeat of that country and the overthrow of the Hitler regime seems to be in sight now and one has the strong impression that the end of the war can only be a matter of weeks.

I am also being given added hope that my departure for England cannot be long delayed. I have a friendly letter from the Bishop of Chichester in which he says:

> I have been in touch with Sir Alexander Maxwell at the Home
> Office about you. He says that they have, as is inevitable, no
> information about you though, of course, they have full particu-
> lars of your father who has a very good reputation, I need
> hardly say, and is much valued as a clergyman and as a friend in
> England.

I am amazed that with all his other commitments the Bishop
takes such an active interest in me, but that is typical of him. I
am very fortunate to have his support.

There are some changes in the office, Mr Lankford who is
my immediate boss – a very pleasant and easy-going man –
leaves and I take over somebody else's work as well. Suddenly
I have quite a volume of work which is a pleasant change. But
the evenings are still free and I always look forward to going
back to the Meyerowitzs' who are so kind and interested in
my life. One evening he gives a private concert for his large
circle of friends. John Millar-Craig comes as well and brings
some of his officer friends with him. The music is again sheer
delight.

For the first time I mention Lt Jerry Dawson, an American
officer in my section. I happen to tell him that my father is in
London. Dawson is due to go to London in a few days' time
and says that he will try and visit my father. In the coming
weeks Jerry Dawson becomes a very kind friend.

In the early days of April I receive a letter from our friends
in Switzerland. I had written to Frau Georg to tell her about
myself and to ask for news about my mother. She now writes
to tell me that after very difficult days my mother is alright
and is staying with her parents in the country. But she has lost
everything. Now I know the best and the worst. It means that
my mother has survived the destruction of Dresden, but also
that we have lost our home there. I am both relieved and
distressed. Ever since the raids on Dresden on 14th February
my anxious thoughts had been with my mother. The uncertainty was the worst, now at least there is news about her. I
write to my father:

> I have been so busy that I have hardly had a minute to myself.
> This is probably just as well. The work has distracted me and
> has helped me to forget for a long time the bad news. Leonie

has lost everything. Poor, poor mother! The first few moments after I received the news were terrible for me. I thought I could not bear it. It was the first time for years that I had to cry. And in those moments I felt very bitter towards God. I could not understand that he did not spare us this blow and that Leonie had to suffer so much. But some hours later I began to realise that we had to be very thankful that she was alive. Of course, those hours when she was bombed out must have been terrible for her and it is sad that the home of my childhood is lost for ever, but the main thing is that she is alive and that the worst is over now. I am much calmer, especially since yesterday afternoon when I prayed with John (Millar-Craig) about it.

On the Sunday after Easter John picks me up again for the service at the PoW Camp. I share with the men in the Sacrament of Holy Communion. I find it a great source of strength. After the service the teacher who seems to act as pastor in the camp asks me for a transcript of my sermon the previous week. He says that it touched on many of their needs and problems. It is encouraging to know that it was a help to some of these troubled men.

Sadly John is given a posting to another part of France and we shall have to say goodbye to one another. I shall miss him very much. He has been a very good and faithful friend. He has made arrangements with an American officer to pick me up every Sunday and to maintain my link with the camp. The arrangement works on the first Sunday after John had gone, but, alas, after that they don't turn up to collect me. I am sorry that this ministry comes to an end. It has meant much to me and I feel that I am letting these prisoners down when they are in such need.

# 8

# Visa Granted

'FRIDAY 13th' has often negative connotations in people's minds, especially if they are superstitious. But for me Friday 13th April 1945 is another Red Letter day. On that day I receive a cable from my father 'Permit granted'. These are two magic words for me. I jump for joy. This is much sooner that I had expected and must be mainly due to the Bishop's intervention. I had vaguely hoped that if all went well I might be in London for my 21st birthday in June. Now this news makes that hope a distinct possibility. All depends, of course, on the French exit visa. If it were not for that hurdle I could be on my way quite soon. Meyerowitz puts a slight damper on my hopes. He comes back from a visit to Paris where he took the trouble to make enquiries about my visa. He was told that in principle no visas will be issued to citizens of enemy countries till after the war. That could still mean a long wait. I tell my father about it:

> I am now a little sad because of the news that Meyerowitz had brought back from Paris. Soon I shall have the British Permit and shall not be able to use it. But I do not despair. Till now I have had success. Why not also for the Visa! I have just come back from town. I saw the British Vice-Consul. He has not yet been advised about the Permit, but thinks that it will arrive within the next few days. I told him about the difficulties with the French Visa and he says that there is nothing he can do about it. I am not very happy because I think it will prove difficult to get the necessary papers. Now before dinner I have just been down to the sea. It is always the best relaxation for me to sit there in the sunshine to look at the blue sea and the wonderful view of the skyline of Marseille. I wish I could share this beautiful scene with you.

On the same day that I receive the goods news of the British Permit the world hears the sad news of the sudden death of the American President Roosevelt. With Churchill and Stalin he was one of the great leaders of the War.

Lt Jerry Dawson returns from London. He has visited my

father and comes back with food and clothes and photos. He now begins to take a personal interest in me and impresses upon me that I must tell him if there is anything I need. I am also transferred to his section in the office where the work is more interesting. But working with the Americans raises another question in my mind which I put to my father:

> I may have the possibility of entering the American Army as an interpreter for the occupation of Germany. I would go then, if they accept me, to Germany in a few months. I am considering it mainly with Leonie (my mother) in mind. Perhaps I could find her and help her, and I think she has more need of me than you. Do you understand? Also supposing the French Visa is not granted or delayed it would then be the best thing for me to do. You understand that I would like to come to you, but if it is not possible for the time being then I would have the chance to go to Germany, to help Leonie and then perhaps to come to England via the US Army.

Fortunately this alternative is overtaken by events and comes to nothing.

26th April is the anniversary of my call-up. I remember standing on the platform in Dresden the previous year and wondering where the train would take us and what would be our fate. How much has happened in this one year is recorded in these pages. Looking back on it now I cannot but marvel that despite all the anxious and critical situations in which I found myself everything has turned out so well. I can see quite clearly the hand of God at work in my life, gently leading me step by step towards freedom and a new life. It is not yet the end of the story, but the end is in sight and with God's help that end will at the same time be a new beginning in England.

Being within sight of the 'finish' I am becoming very unsettled and frustrated now. Time seems to stand still and officialdom stands in the way of getting out of France. Several times I call at the British Consulate to find out whether my Permit has arrived, but I am just too impatient.

On the war front events move now with dramatic speed. Each day reports the fall of more German towns. There is now hard fighting in Berlin itself. Mussolini is assassinated by Italian partisans. On 2nd May it is reported that Hitler has died or committed suicide in the Chancellery in Berlin. I can hardly believe it yet. This dictator who has dominated our lives for twelve long years is no more. Admiral Doenitz is now in supreme command in Germany. The following day it is announced that Berlin has fallen to the Russians. The chaos and destruction of Germany is by all accounts beyond description. On 7th May we hear in the afternoon that Doenitz has announced the capitulation of Germany. In the evening special editions of the papers report that at 14.00 hours General Jodl has signed the unconditional surrender of all German forces at Eisenhower's Headquarters in Rheims. Thus ends the Second World War, a global conflict on a monumental scale. One forgets at this moment that the war with Japan in the Far East is still going on, but for us in Europe it is over. For me personally it is the end of twelve years of suffering and discrimination, twelve long years which – as I reflect in my diary – have cost me my youth. But now I can look forward to the future which I hope may in some measure compensate for some of the evils of the past. I also make the comment that what may seem God's judgment on the nations may open the eyes of mankind to the revelation of God in Jesus Christ. I kept a French newspaper cutting of that historic day which sums up the situation in Germany.

> Factories destroyed, the male population either dead or captured, all semblance of government gone, a bleak depressing future ahead. Ruin and destruction everywhere, a terrifying defeat. Such is the balance sheet of the Nazi regime. The catastrophe of Germany is without precedent in history.

I write to my father on that day:

> It is a wonderful feeling that the war is over. After so many years I can hardly believe it. Now we will pray to God that he will give us new strength so that we can build a new life and a new home for the three of us. I am only sorry because I had hoped that I could celebrate this day with you. For us V-Day will come only when I can embrace you and know that I am at last with you. Here flags fly from all houses and last night, after the first news of the end of the war came through, many people crowded the streets of the city and cheered.

On Tuesday, 8th May at 3.00 pm the sirens sound all over Marseille, the bells ring, young people roam through the streets shouting and celebrating. Henry picks me up from the office in his Jeep to drive us through the streets and join in the victory celebrations. Everywhere flags and buntings are out. The Canebiere, the main thoroughfare of Marseille, is jammed with people. We can hardly move. France has a public holiday. And the weather is festive, too. Hot and sunny. A few days later I write to England:

> Did I tell you that on V-Day in the evening Henry picked me up with two Americans and we drove round the town, through crowds full of exuberance. Then we went to the most prominent site in Marseille – the Notre Dame Church. It stands on a hill. We looked down on all the lights of the festive city.

To add to the general joyful atmosphere there is a note from the British Consulate. They confirm that the British Visa has been granted, but it is subject to the issue of the French Exit Visa. Immediately I go on to the Passport Office who say that once my application has been filed it might take 4–6 weeks. At least they don't rule out the possibility of issuing the Visa. I am sent to the Police Section for Foreigners where my particulars are taken down for the official investigation of my application. Well, now it is in the pipeline and I must wait and hope. With the end of the war the Americans are scaling down their operations and I wonder whether this will affect me –

> I was a little afraid that because of the end of the war the Americans would pay off the civilians and would close the office. But Lt Dawson has assured me that for the next few months there is no danger of that happening and that as long as there is a job for him there will be also one for me. The heat is dreadful (I write on 14th May). I am always thirsty and always drinking. Last night I was in the sea for a swim, just across the road, and today after work I shall do the same again.

In the same letter there are also some reflections on past and future –

> With God's help we shall begin a new life which will be as good or even better than it was before. I think it will be better because we know only now what it means 'to live'. We have learned that not everything must be as it is, but that we have to open our eyes and then everything is of God's grace. That is the good thing that has come out of the hard times that we have

been through; that we have a deeper knowledge of God, his power and his miracles. Hard times have brought us nearer to him. For that we have to be thankful.

On Whit Sunday, Henry and I are invited to Mme Morosov, a Russian emigre. She works at the American stores. One evening she has to work late and Henry is assigned to take her home in the Jeep. When she discovers that he is German she asks Henry to stop the car and let her get out. She does not want to have anything to do with a 'boche'. Henry must have talked her round and reassured her. In fact, when they get to her home she invites him to stay for dinner. Her husband is Russian as well. From this chance meeting develops a close friendship and Henry is practically adopted as their son. In due course Henry (who now shares a room with me at the Meyerowitzs') moves to them and lives there until he leaves France in 1947. The Morosovs are a delightful couple, especially Madame. We spend a most enjoyable evening with them and return several times to enjoy their hospitality.

During May I receive a letter from my father with news from my mother. An American officer has written to him. Together with her parents and sister my mother is somewhere in Central Germany, in the American Sector. The news gives us new hope. If she is in the American sector there may be a good chance of getting her out. Perhaps before long all three of us will be reunited. Alas, this hope does not materialise. A week or two later there is a letter from her from Coburg. She sounds desperate. They are very hungry and she pleads for help. What can we do? Jerry Dawson, now a 1st Lieutenant, offers to write a letter on my behalf to Lt Aronson, the American officer, to ask for his help. But by the time this letter is written the area where my mother lives with her parents is ceded to the Russians. They are not allowed to leave with the American Forces to the new demarcation line. They are stranded in the Russian Zone in much more unpleasant conditions. Naturally, our contact with her breaks off and we are left in complete ignorance about her fate. In the coming weeks and months this is a great anxiety for us. Eventually she is repatriated to West Germany via Berlin. But we have to wait for another year before that happens.

My next letter to my father is in German. An American

from the office is visiting London and will post my letter there. There is a good reason why I don't want to send this letter through the normal mail. At long last I have the chance to tell my father about a predicament that has been worrying me ever since I first applied for the French Visa:

> I have already warned you that I might not be given the French Visa. When I came to Marseille and later had to obtain legitimate papers the Comite where I was working submitted on my behalf a false statement to the Prefecture. The statement said that I had emigrated to France in 1939, had remained there, had been in several camps and had finally been sent to the Todt Organization for forced labour. That was the only way to get a resident's Permit for Marseille, which I still have and which has to be extended at the Prefecture each month. Had they known the truth they would have put me in a Prisoner-of-War camp regardless of my special background. Now, of course, they will investigate my case in connection with my application for the Visa and I fear that they may discover the truth. In that case, I shall be in trouble. I hope that my luck will hold. So far everything has worked out incredibly well. But I have no illusions and must be prepared for the worst. If you knew what miracles I have encountered since my escape you would be amazed. You won't believe it when I tell you about them one day. But you will understand that as long as I am in France and am only free because of this fictitious story I feel unsettled.

However, Meyerowitz raises my hopes about this Visa. He manages to have a word with the Director of the Passport Office who refers him to the Police where fortunately again he knows somebody. Through his intervention my dossier will now be sent to Paris. I am so lucky. Without his help my application would probably remain in the 'In' tray indefinitely because the authorities don't really know anything about me and are not interested in my case.

When I return from work on Monday, 18th June there is a note from the Prefecture 'VISA GRANTED'. I am speechless. I dare not believe it until I have it confirmed. Dear Jean Meyerowitz rushes immediately to the Prefecture, but the office is already closed. I can hardly settle to anything for the rest of the day. I am so excited and dumbfounded. I don't get much sleep that night, my mind is racing in anticipation. Next morning I rush to the Prefecture as soon as they open and they

confirm the note. It really is true! The moment that I have
been waiting for and that only a few months ago seemed
almost unattainable has come. I was quite resigned to the fact
that the French visa would take a long time and that I might
be in France for another few months. Now suddenly overnight
I can think of packing my bags . . .

> The greatest surprise has happened, the great day is here. The
> Visa is granted! I cannot quite believe this latest miracle that
> God has given me, and yet it is true. When I came home last
> night I found on my bed a note from the Passport Office to call
> there because 'Visa accorde'. For the first moment I could not
> think at all. Then I thought – no, that must be a mistake. The
> application has only been forwarded to Paris on Wednesday of
> last week and this note from the Passport Office was written on
> Friday and arrived here yesterday. There is only one possibility,
> i.e. that Pastor Boegner (head of the French Protestant Church)
> has intervened without waiting for the arrival of my papers and
> that he has been successful.
>
> Can you understand that this seems like a gift from heaven?
> Can you imagine that since last night I seem to be more in
> heaven than on earth? I slept only two or three hours last night.
> Thousands of thoughts kept going through my mind. I had
> assumed, that at the earliest I might leave her in August and
> now I hope to be reunited with you within the next two weeks.
> I hope to arrive in England before the end of June. Could God
> have given me a better birthday present than this (my 21st
> birthday was on 21st June).
>
> Now as for my plans. I went to the Passport Office this
> morning, had to complete some formalities and shall get the
> Visa and travel papers tomorrow morning. Then I shall go to
> the British Consulate and hope to get the British Visa straighta-
> way. And then I am ready to leave. But although I don't want to
> lose one minute to join you, I would like to spend my birthday
> with Henry and Meyerowitz. And I need to say goodbye to a
> few people and do my packing. And last, but not least, I have to
> wait for a lift to Paris which the Americans will arrange and
> which will be much better than going by train. Lt Dawson will
> see to it that I get some transport at the first possible opportu-
> nity. As soon as I am in Paris and know when I leave there and
> arrive at an English port (Newhaven?) I will send you a telegram.
> I hope and pray that there will no difficulties at the last moment
> and that I shall arrive in England at the end of next week.

Two days later I collect both the French and British Visas and also the French safe-conduit which I need for travelling in France (before I was confined to Marseille). I don't quite make it for my 21st birthday in England. But that does not matter now. Instead I celebrate my birthday on the beach in glorious sunshine. In the evening I have a lovely meal with the Meyerowitzs'. At my special request he plays the Moonlight Sonata for me.

Dawson very kindly arranges Army transport for me to Paris. The Maitre invites me Meyerowitz and Henry for a last sumptious meal. I say goodbye in the office and to Meyerowitz and Henry. With a heavy heart I part from Henry. We have been through so much together and have been almost like brothers. I hate to leave him behind. I remember very little about the last few days in France. I must have been in a constant daze. I think I went to see the Marchant-Hacots whom I had not seen since those first days of our freedom at the Chapelotte.

The British Consulate in Paris gives me special authorization for the ferry from Dieppe to Newhaven which is still run by the military authorities. On Thursday 28th June I arrive in Newhaven, probably the first enemy alien to invade Great Britain! The moment I leave France and step on to British soil an enormous burden is lifted from my mind. Right up to the last moment I fear that something might go wrong or hold me up. As I have intimated before, I worried that the French might find out that I had made a false statement and might stop me from leaving the country. Now for the first time I feel completely free. It is an overwhelming moment when we approach the English coast.

The formalities in Newhaven don't take long. I feel at once that England is home for me and that I am safe and secure here. Hours later I arrive at Victoria Station. When I step onto the platform my father walks past me. He does not recognise me. I was a boy of 14 when he left us. I am a man of 21 when we meet again over six years later. A long dream (sometimes a nightmare) has become reality. I step into a new life.

# 9

# Reflections

WHEN my father left us for England in March 1939 none of us would have guessed that six months later Germany would be at war with Britain and that the war would go on for six long years. There had been several political crises before which could have led to armed conflict, but in the end they were averted. We still believed that nobody wanted war. Even well in 1939 we were not prepared to take the threat of war seriously, certainly not within a matter of months. As I mentioned before, even in July and August of that year my mother was still planning to visit my father in England in September. This was to be a preliminary visit prior to us joining him there permanently as soon as possible. I believe my father had already made enquiries about a school for me. And then on 3rd September the blow fell. War was declared and at least for the time being our hope of moving to England was suddenly dashed. Even then we still thought that both sides would pull back from the brink. We certainly never expected a long drawn out conflict. Instead it took over six years before I saw my father again and before my dream of one day arriving in England was fulfilled.

Suddenly I woke up and indeed it was true! I was really in Newhaven, at Victoria Station, at Walham Green in London. My father was a Curate in Fulham and lived in digs off Walham Green – a small study and a small bedroom. Mrs Smith was the landlady who gave me a wonderful welcome. For a year I shared the small bedroom with my father. It was a squash, but we managed. In 1946 my mother arrived from Germany and we moved into a small flat almost next door to the Church – Christ Church, Fulham.

When I was reunited with my father there was so much to talk about, so much for me to tell which I had not been able to say in my letters. But I also had to take stock of my life. Now I had peace of mind to look back over these six years and especially over the last year which had been such a tremendous upheaval. When I got on that train on 26th April 1944 none of us in that mixed company had any idea where we were going, what we would be doing, how we would be treated, whether we would survive, and if we did, where we were going to land up at the end. But then gradually there were certain landmarks, bigger and smaller ones which stood out and which when pieced together amounted to some providence which I could only call divine.

There was the chance meeting with a family friend at the transit camp in Paris who advised me to join the technical unit. Had I been at the Atlantic Coast and right in the forefront of the Allied invasion I might not have survived. There was the meeting with Henry on the emergency train which led to a friendship and mutual support through thick and thin right to the day I left Marseille (we did lose touch when he went to the States in 1947, but many years later when he was on a business trip to London he found my name in the telephone directory and we met again and renewed our friendship until his sad death from cancer in September 1992). There was the foolhardy jump from the train when we were being pulled back to Germany, with the Allied forces close on our heels. That could have gone disastrously wrong in which case we would have been shot on the spot. It was a desperate bid for freedom and mercifully it succeeded. And then there was the most desperate moment in my life when I was taken into the fortress in Marseille and was enlisted into the French Foreign Legion and all my hope of getting to England would have been dashed to pieces, at least for the next five years. And there and then the greatest miracle of all, what I can only call divine intervention when just as speedily I was delivered from the Legion. That became quite clearly the biggest landmark in my life. I could not have engineered it. Humanly speaking, I could not get out of the fortress once I was in. I was trapped. I have no other explanation for that extraordinary and uncanny release and its precise timing but a supernatural rescue. The profound effect of that event on my life subsequently stands to reason.

The next big landmark with far-reaching results was the opportunity to preach for the first time in that Prisoner-of-War Camp. Who would have guessed that this opportunity would come my way! Humanly speaking, very unlikely. But a British Army Chaplain turns up and needs somebody who speaks German to assist him in his services. And there and then my heart was strangely warmed (to use John Wesley's famous phrase) and I began to wonder, was this possibly what God was calling me to?

Then there was the Bishop of Chichester who took the time and trouble to intercede for me with the British authorities. There was Jean Meyerowitz who so generously offered me a home. There was Jerry Dawson, the Lieutenant who took me under his wings. There was, of course, my father who once we had established contact moved heaven and earth to encourage me and bring me to this country. And there was the mysterious final intervention which to this day I don't know who to attribute it to – when quite unexpectedly and much sooner than could reasonably be expected the French Exit Visa was 'accorde'. I still wonder who made that possible.

In the midst of adversity there were all along the way these landmarks, big and small. I would have been very blind if I had not taken note of them. In the end they all added up to one clear conclusion – that someone's guiding hand was upon me. And to me that guiding hand was not chance or coincidence, but GOD. There was no other possible explanation that made any sense to me.

I suppose it is fair to say that I was brought up in Germany in a conventional Christian home. I was encouraged in Forst to go to the 'Kindergottesdienst', the Children's Service. Later I used to go with my father to a Church where the Pastor belonged to the Confessional Church which defied Hitler. When I moved to Dresden I joined the Confirmation Class and came under the influence of a very impressive Christian Minister. And in April 1939 I was confirmed by him. But over against that there were these nagging questions for which there seemed to be no answer – Why did I have to have a non-Aryan stigma attached to my life? Why could I not be like all the other boys whose apparently carefree upbringing I envied? Why did I have to go through the humiliating experience when my classmates branded me openly as a Jew? Why was our family troubled with anxiety and uncertainty about the future? Why could I not go to University and study for a degree and for an interesting professional job? And why was I eventually called up for forced labour? All these questions were adding up to the one burning and agonizing question 'Why did God allow all this to happen?' Why were we, why was I afflicted with this adversity? What was the point of it, why had I deserved such a fate?

Although I had had a Christian upbringing it was not strong enough to counteract all these questions about a good and loving God. My faith was still rather nominal and conventional and could not cope with the knocks I was about to take. It was in this vulnerable state that I was plunged into the experience of forced labour in France. Physically I was fit, but in these circumstances I did not feel safe. Anything could happen to me at any moment. I began to realise that despite my religious upbringing, despite my Confirmation I did not have the inner resources to stand up to the precarious conditions in which I found myself. But 'man's extremity is God's opportunity'. During those long months in France I became receptive to God's dealings with me. I don't think it was so much that I suddenly remembered that I needed God's help – although I am sure that was a factor in my perplexity – it was much more that I became aware of these 'nudgings', of these strange interventions in my adversity. I became aware of a power other than my own which was with me and overruled, sometimes in the most bizarre and unpromising situations. I suppose it is true to say that as I experienced these remarkable turning points I was gradually being 'converted' to God. These moments turned me to God in a much more radical way than I had ever known before.

The great lesson that I learnt during this time and that has stayed with me ever since is that adversity, suffering, need does not have to be negative and destructive. God can use it to bring something good and creative out of it. It reminds me of the reply which Joseph gave to his brothers after he had been through his afflictions 'You meant to do me harm, but God meant to bring good out of it'. I would not have chosen to go through the unhappy experiences of the Nazi regime, I would not have chosen forced labour in France, but as it came my way I can now look back on it as a painful, but redemptive transformation of my life. Without wanting to boast about it it has given me a deeper understanding of suffering and insight into other people's troubles and agonies which I could not have found in any other way. When I arrived in England on that 28th June 1945 I knew God in a new way, or rather God in his mercy had made himself known to me. I have sometimes facetiously said that I owe it to Hitler that I came to Christ. That is a very facile way of saying that the persecution of the Hitler years has had the effect of leading me to faith in Jesus Christ.

I remember that in the early days after my arrival in England I was given the opportunity of making a definite response to what God had done for me. There was at that time a well-known evangelist, Lindsay Glegg. He came to the YMCA in Fulham and my father and I went to one of his meetings. I did not go forward at the end of the evening as some others did. But I know that in my heart I made a solemn decision that evening that I wanted to give my life to Christ and serve him in his Church. I have always been glad that Lindsay Glegg gave me this opportunity. It was, in a way, the climax of all that had gone before. It gave expression to the spiritual journey that I had made. From now on I was set on a new quest, that of serving Christ within his Church. I was not quite sure yet how this was going to be fulfilled, but a new chapter in my life had begun.

The second part of this book will relate how God led me on from these war time experiences to a very rewarding and fulfilling life at home and abroad.

PART TWO

# 10

# Training for the Ministry and Curacy (1948–1955)

'GOD moves in a mysterious way his wonders to perform'. I never thought when I left Germany in April 1944 that fourteen months later I would be in England hoping to be ordained in the Anglican Church. Those fourteen months at the time seemed like eternity, but what are fourteen months in the course of a lifetime. And yet, how much had happened to me during that period and how amazingly formative it had proved to be. God had certainly performed his wonders in a mysterious way. And now I was anxious to pursue this way, *his* way further. I realised that entering the Anglican ministry, if I was admitted at all, would not be happening overnight. I would still have to overcome a number of hurdles and at each hurdle I could easily be eliminated. My knowledge of English was by no means fluent (I had come over with an American accent after working in the office in Marseille). I needed to adjust to the English way of life. I had to qualify educationally for any academic training. My father could not support me financially for any length of time. I was given to understand that the British Permit was issued on the understanding that I would find a job that would contribute to the war effort. And although the actual war was now over in Europe Britain was still on a war footing.

One of the first steps I had to take was to look for such a job which would also mean earning some money. A friend of my father's who was a director of a company offered me a job in his firm as a filing clerk. So I cycled from Fulham to Wimbledon every day to earn my living. The job was not particularly exciting, but I like being methodical and it was important to file correspondence under the right letter or heading.

Next in order to qualify at all for the possibility of theological training I had to retake my matriculation. My German 'Abitur' was not valid in this country. I enrolled in a Wolsey Hall Correspondence Course and when I came home from the office worked very hard every evening in order to take the London University Entrance Examination.

On my first Sunday in London I went to my father's Church in Fulham. It was my first experience of worshipping in an Anglican Church. I was made very welcome and felt immediately at home in the Prayer Book liturgy. My only shock that morning was when the tune of the first hymn was the German National Anthem. However, I was reassured when the words we sang were 'Glorious things of thee are spoken'! Very quickly I got involved in the worship and activities of Christ Church, Fulham. I also began to appreciate the importance of both Word and Sacrament. I had been a Lutheran and had been confirmed in the Lutheran Church. If I wanted to apply for the ordained ministry in the Church of England I first needed to be a full member of that Church. That meant being confirmed as an Anglican. When I expressed my dilemma of being confirmed a second time my very wise Vicar put my mind at rest and said that I should regard this Confirmation as becoming a member of another family within the worldwide Christian community. So I was duly confirmed by the Bishop of Kensington.

The next step was to find out whether I would be considered for training for the ministry. I went to see Kenneth Carey who was then General Secretary of CACTM (Church's Advisory Council for the Training for the Ministry) who later became Bishop of Edinburgh. He said something to me that I have remembered ever since. I was then fully involved in the Youth Group of my Church. But I had developed a duodenal ulcer probably as a result of the stress and poor diet in France. This meant that I had to have some treatment and had to drop out of everything for two or three months. I bemoaned this fact when I talked to Carey and must have said to him that I wondered how the Youth Group would manage without me. Carey looked at me and said 'Simonson, do you think that you are indispensable?' How right he was! However, he put me forward for a Selection Conference at Warminster. I cannot remember much about it, but I was accepted for training. Having been a Selector myself I am still amazed that the Selectors then saw fit to recommend me. I first had to pass the London University Entrance Examination. This meant another delay before I could actually commence my training.

In the meantime I found another job at Cluttons, the Surveyors of the Ecclesiastical Commissioners (now Church Commissioners) where I had a dull job checking piles of War Damage schedules. But at least I earned £4 a week which for me was a great deal of money. Being a very keen Christian I wondered whether I could start a Bible Study Group in the office. I went to see the firm's Secretary, a very pleasant man, and asked for permission. He turned it down very gently by saying 'I am afraid, Mr Simonson, business and religion don't go together'.

In July 1946, a year after me, my mother arrived in England. Through the intervention of Probst Grueber, the Dean of the Church in Berlin, she was able to get out of the Russian Zone and go to West Germany. After some time, again with the help of the Bishop of Chichester, she was reunited with us in London. That in itself was a miracle. She could have perished in Dresden, my father was in London when the doodle-bugs were dropped on the capital, and I could have landed up in the French Foreign Legion. But through God's providence all three of us were reunited again after seven long years. We set up a new home in a small flat almost next door to the Church in Fulham.

Soon after my arrival I had met the Bishop of Chichester. Later I went down to Hove to meet him again at the Diocesan Church House. What impressed me most and what has stayed in my mind were his beautiful translucent blue eyes. I felt that I was in the presence of a man of God.

My father belonged to the British-German Christian Fellowship which had been able to operate right through the war and had the Bishop of Chichester as its Patron. I went with my father to some of their meetings. We heard Martin Niemoeller, one of the leaders of the Confessional Church in Germany who had survived Concentration Camp, when he preached soon after the war in Holy Trinity, Brompton. In the congregation were many English people who did not understand German. Speaking to some of them after the service they said that they had been so impressed by his personality that they could almost understand his message. I went to another meeting at which the speakers were Bishop Hans Lilje, another leader of the Confessional Church, and Professor Gordon Rupp, a Methodist theologian. Gordon Rupp had a very lean figure whereas Lilje was almost tubby. Those of us who did not know these gentlemen assumed that Rupp was Lilje who had come out of starving Germany and Lilje was the English theologian who had been better nourished.

For my theological training I would have preferred to go to Ridley Hall, Cambridge where my father had been. But taking the London University Entrance Examination (which I passed in due course) tied me to a College affiliated to London University. The choice was between Oakhill and the London College of Divinity. The latter could offer me the London B.D. Course. I was also offered a place. In October 1948 I moved there from Dalston where shortly before my father had become Vicar of St Mark's. The London College of Divinity, formerly St John's, had to leave Highbury during the war and eventually found a new home at Ford Manor at Dormansland in Surrey. The Manor belonged to Mrs Spender-Clay who in turn was related to the Bowes-Lyons, the present Queen Mother's family. There right out in the country in the main building and some further outbuildings room was found for some forty students and a permanent Staff of five. The Principal was Dr Donald Coggan, later to become Archbishop of Canterbury. He had assembled a very able team as his staff. Ralph Dean was the Vice-Principal. He later became Bishop of Cariboo in Canada and then well known as Executive Officer of the Anglican Communion. Douglas Webster was still in his twenties when he was appointed as Tutor in Doctrine. He later became Theologian Missioner for CMS and travelled round the world. Finally he was one of the Residentiary Canons at St Paul's Cathedral. He also wrote a number of stimulating books on Mission. Bob Hooper taught us the Old Testament. David Brown who had recently been a student also joined the Staff part-time to teach New Testament Greek and Hebrew. He later became Principal of the Theological College at Mundri in the Sudan and eventually was made Bishop of Guildford. Very sadly he died prematurely. Quite a number of the students had recently come out of the Forces where some of them had been officers. One of them had only been converted a short time before he came to LCD and had a very scanty knowledge of the Christian Faith and of the Bible. On the first day of term we all had to sit a Bible Paper to show some evidence how much (or how little) we knew of the Scriptures. The new convert gave up after a few minutes and spent the next three hours writing a number of personal letters instead. He caught up very quickly in the following weeks.

The peaceful rural setting in which we lived as a community with a daily time-table of lectures and worship and reading proved very conducive to our spiritual growth. Each term we had a Quiet Day when a Conductor would lead our thinking and praying. In the first term we had Clifford Martin, the Bishop of Liverpool, who took three verses from II Timothy 1. Here was another man of God whose spiritual stature made a deep impression on me. I was to hear and meet him again on other occasions.

We all had to do some pastoral work in the Churches and parishes around the College. A number of us were sent to the Epileptic Colony, as it was then called, at Lingfield, near the Racecourse. Two of us visited one of the homes there and took services for the patients. Quite often, in the middle of the service, one or the other of the patients would suddenly pass out. One of the male nurses would attend to him. We would carry on with the service.

My interest in the Healing Ministry began here. When we had visited that home for some time and prayed with the patients and read the Bible with them we were told by the Warden that on the nights when we had been there the chaps had fewer fits than at other times. The calming influence of the presence of Christ through the Word and through prayer had a definite effect on their bodies. Our tutor, Douglas Webster, started up a Healing Prayer Group in the College which some of us attended. This was in the early days of the revival of the Healing Ministry in the Church and I have been grateful ever since that there my concern for Christian Healing was kindled. Another concern which later led to service over-seas was introduced by the Vigiles Society in the College. This existed to support the missionary work of the Church by

prayer and information. Once a week the Secretary of the
Society would come round and firmly knock on our doors to
wake us up. 'Vigiles' met before Chapel, round about 7 am.
Needless to say, some would turn over and go back to sleep
for another half an hour. Those of us who went would pray
for some part of the missionfield. Sometimes we would even
have a speaker or a missionary who was home on furlough.
My interest in Mission and especially in the work of the
Church Missionary Society was nurtured here.

A third concern which has continued throughout my ministry was evangelism. Each year, usually during the Easter Vacation, the College conducted a Mission, sometimes jointly with
students from CMS. These would be well prepared with
preliminary meetings at the College or visits to the parish
concerned. The Mission that has stayed clearly in my mind
was at St Helens in Lancashire. We were divided up between
the large Parish Church and the two or three daughter
churches. Each morning we had a briefing session at which it
was decided what each of us would do on that day. Often it
meant door to door visiting. There were visits to schools,
clubs, house groups, children's meetings. And in the evenings
there were Mission Services with testimonies, invitations to
make a decision for Christ and counselling afterwards. Bishop
Martin of Liverpool commissioned us at the beginning of the
Mission and gave each one of us a word as he passed along the
Communion rail. At that time I was still a little tongue-tied in
English. The verse the Bishop gave me was Matthew 10.19:
'Take no thought how and what ye shall speak, for it shall be
given you in that same hour what ye shall speak'. It was a
great encouragement to me. In fact, I was asked to give my
testimony at one of the Mission Services in the packed Church.
I was very nervous, but I remembered the word that I had
been given.

In those days St Helen's had a famous Men's Bible Class.
Up to 500 men met each Sunday afternoon in the Parish
Church. It was an amazing sight seeing all these men hearing
and studying the Word of God together. Those were the days!
Alas, those days have gone. I believe that the Men's Bible
Class does not exist any more.

The same is true of the great Missionary Rallies that I

attended in those days. CMS used to fill the Empress Hall in Kensington to capacity. It was quite a sight seeing one coachload after another from all parts of Southern England arriving and thousands of faithful missionary supporters pouring into that vast hall. And then the long procession of Bishops and missionary leaders mounting the platform. Again of all the speakers I remember clearly Clifford Martin giving the final message at one of these annual rallies with just two words from the Crucifixion 'One ran . . .' And then the whole audience of 10,000 people rose as one man to sing the final hymn 'Lift high the Cross'. You could argue that the Church was too triumphant in those days but in these days of small things these are precious memories.

Each year the College used to send a group of students on a Church Army Evangelistic Weekend. We were based at the Headquarters at Bryanstone Square near Marble Arch. We were given talks on Evangelism and then on Saturday afternoon Captain Coll would march us to Speakers' Corner where Church Army had a stand. One by one we were shoved up to the soapbox. We felt like lambs being led to the slaughter and, to change the metaphor, we all had butterflies in our tummies. But there was no escape. You stood your ground for five minutes delivering your message and ignored the catcalls from down below. You felt greatly relieved when you came down. But that was not all. When we had finished at Hyde Park Corner we marched back to Edgware Road and spread out to do 'fishing'. This meant engaging any passer-by in conversation and inviting him or her to a Mission Service in the Chapel of Church Army HQ. We did not 'catch' many, but a few came and heard the Gospel. It was all straight from the shoulder, but for all its ordeal it taught us some down-to-earth evangelism. I doubt whether one could go about it in quite the same way today. Evangelism, Overseas Mission and Healing were three of the important influences on my life which first impressed me at College and have remained with me since. Later Ecumenism became another one.

Back at College it was not all work, but also some play. We worked and studied hard, but we also had our fun and relaxation. Especially in spring and summer the Surrey countryside was beautiful and on Saturday afternoons some of us would get on our bikes and cycle to Edenbridge or Oxted or East Grinstead to do our shopping. There used to be also healthy warfare between us and our sister College, Oakhill in Southgate. We would have the occasional nightly raid on the other College. I remember one night when Oakhill walked off with two precious statues which, of course, did not belong to the College, but to Mrs Spender-Clay, our landlady, who lived in one part of the building. Needless to say, she was not too pleased. There was a great commotion, frantic phone calls to Oakhill and a rather penitent carload of students from there returning the booty.

Sunday evenings we would often go and worship at our Parish Church at Dormansland where the Vicar was Canon Edge-Partington. We knew him better under the name of Buff-Orpington! We worshipped with the village folk. The gentry went to Church in the morning.

In the summer of 1951 I went for the first time to Lee Abbey in North Devon. Lee Abbey had been founded by Roger de Pemberton as a venture of faith after the war. He had found a real gem of a place. The house and grounds stood on the edge of the magnificent Devon coastline. At the bottom of the hill is a lovely bay for swimming and all along the coast are many walks with glorious views of the coast and the sea. Lee Abbey was and still is a centre for holidays and Christian renewal. Many people of all ages, but especially the younger generation, have found there a vision of Christ and of his Church. When I went Geoffrey Rogers was the Warden. He had been a missionary in Iran. He had great gifts of leadership and determination. He led a community, mainly young people, who ran the house and the estate. Among his team was Jack Winslow who again had been a missionary in India. He was now almost seventy and with the wisdom of old age was a spiritual counsellor to many people. He was also a poet and hymn-writer. To him we owe the great hymn 'Lord of all power, I give you my will' (AMNS 395). In the evenings in the Octagonal Lounge there were epilogues, usually with an evangelistic note. Students and nurses formed a large part of this houseparty that I attended that summer. I went back a year later and with Jack Winslow took part in a service which was broadcast on BBC Radio.

In 1951 I met Jean there. She was a nurse at St Bartholomew's Hospital in London. When we parted at the end of the houseparty I said to her that we must meet again. I went first to a SCM Conference in Bangor and then on a visit to some of my relatives in Germany. I wrote to Jean from there and contacted her as soon as I came back. When I was back at College we used to meet at Godstone. She came down on the Green Line and we went for long walks. In November on a wet night I proposed to her in St James' Park and we got engaged.

In June 1952 during a very hot week I took the exams for a London B.D. Our Old Testament Tutor, Bob Hooper, had become Vicar of Midhurst by then and Jean was down there helping Mary Hooper with her young family. As soon as I had finished the exams I dashed down to Midhurst. After weeks of swotting and apprehension I could now relax. My College days or rather years, four in all, came to an end. I made a number of good friends. Graeme Spiers, later Archdeacon of Liverpool, became my best man and also godfather to our son.

The spiritual influence that the College had exercised on us under the strong leadership of Dr Coggan laid a solid foundation for my future ministry. I remember that when I went to see him to tell him of our engagement he asked me 'Does she love the Lord ten times as much as you do?' She did.

Coggan had been to a Church in Kilburn to preach and when he came back he called me in to say that the new Vicar there was in need of a Curate for that large and demanding parish. Would I like to have a look at the parish and meet the Vicar. Raleigh Prater had himself been the Curate there and when the Vicar left was asked to succeed him. That was fairly unusual. It was a parish of about 40,000 people, mainly working class and artisans. The main Church, St Luke's near Queen's Park Station, had been bombed in the war. The services were now held at St Simon's. There was also a daughter Church, St Jude's. It was quite a daunting proposition to go to such a tough parish. We thought about it and prayed about it, and said 'yes'. I went to see Dr Wand, the Bishop of London, or rather the Lord Bishop of London for in those days the Bishop was still a very lordly figure. I felt in fear and trembling of him when I entered his study in Fulham Palace. However, he was very gracious and offered me a title and a lordly stipend of £400. That was a concession because we were soon to be married. The basic stipend for Curates was then £300.

I had to sit for the Deacon's examination at Fulham Palace to prove my worth. Having sat a number of exams at College and then the marathon of the London B.D. with about eight papers within a week, it seemed rather odd to take yet one more exam. On Monday 11th August I rushed to Senate House, Kensington where the results of the London B.D. were posted and was greatly relieved and delighted that my name was among the Passes. I had hoped for an Honours Degree, but considering that I had only arrived seven years earlier in this country I was quite content that I had got a degree at all. I hardly had time to celebrate this good news for on the following day was our wedding.

Jean had qualified as a State Registered Nurse in 1952. She would have gone on to Midwifery training, but I appeared on the scene and marriage intervened. During the engagement we had met as often as we could. During the vacations when I was at Dalston where my father was now Vicar she used to come over or I would met her at Barts' Hospital. Now the great day of our wedding dawned. Graeme Spiers, my best man, came over to Dalston to pick me up and escort me to Wandsworth Common, Jean's home. The marriage took place at St Mary Magdalen, Trinity Road. Three clergy took part in the service – my father who married us, Donald Coggan who gave the address, and Piers Goulding, the Vicar who took only a minor part. Unfortunately, Coggan had almost lost his voice and could only speak with difficulties. Jean's bridesmaids were Pam Shorter and Connie Crane, both now also married for many years. We still see them and Graeme Spiers from time to time and all three joined us for the celebration of our 40th wedding anniversary last year.

After the service we had the reception at Jean's home just across the Common. There was a marquee in the garden, the usual speeches and photos and then we set off for our honeymoon in Cornwall.

On our return we moved into our first home. It was a small flat in a condemned house next door to the Church Hall in Denmark Road, Kilburn. Out of our modest stipend we had to pay rent for the flat. Within a radius of about 100 yards there were five pubs. Particularly on Fridays nights after payday it was very rowdy. Even when the pubs closed down at 11 pm parties would adjourn to houses down the road and would carry on till the early hours of the morning. In those days there were no licensed betting shops. The bookie used to go from door to door to collect the bets. Often we had the bookie's watcher on our doorstep. Whenever the police approached the watcher would call out 'taxi' and the bookie would disappear in the home of the nearest client and make his exit through their back garden. Our flat was on the second floor. Our only garden was a window box. It was a corner house and from our living room we had a good view of the goings-on down below.

At Michaelmas 1952 I was made deacon by the Bishop of London at the ordination at St Paul's Cathedral. It was an awe-inspiring occasion. There were about forty of us, priests and deacons. In those days there were large numbers of ordinations. There was no manpower problem in the Church. The supply of candidates, especially of men who had been demobilised after the end of the war, was more than adequate. One was normally expected to serve two curacies before one was considered for a living.

I remember a slightly delicate issue at our ordination. We were expected to wear a stole, but there were a few candidates from evangelical Colleges like Oakhill who regarded a stole as 'popish' and refused to wear it. For them a doctrinal issue was at stake. Right up to the last minute there was some doubt whether the Bishop of London would ordain them, but in the end they were. The London College of Divinity was also evangelical and we had among our number some who were very Protestant. But on the whole the ethos of the College was that of a reasonable evangelicalism which I appreciated. The wearing of a stole was not an issue for me and I was quite content to wear it at St Paul's. Back at Kilburn it was black scarf. It was a parish under the auspices of the Church Pastoral Aid Society.

At the retreat preceding the ordination two or three of us strayed from the straight and narrow path. The Retreat was held at St Edwards House Westminster which belonged to the

Cowley Fathers. Later I had a high regard for this community which I met again in the States. But in those early days I was not yet used to High Church practices and found the incense and the number of offices too oppressive One of us had noticed in the papers that Professor James S. Stewart, the great Scottish divine, was preaching at the City Temple on the Sunday morning. We sneaked out of St Edward's House and heard a most eloquent and uplifting sermon which I think made a valid contribution to our retreat. We slipped back unnoticed and were in our places for lunch.

Michaelmas Day was on a Monday. After the Ordination both our parents took us out to lunch somewhere near St Paul's and then Jean and I went back to Kilburn. Talk about being dropped in at the deep end! Every Monday evening was a Women's Service at St Simon's. I was emotionally drained after an awe-inspiring service at St Paul's Cathedral. But my Vicar suggested that I should make my first appearance in the parish at this evening service. I had to say a few words to introduce myself, but at least I was not expected to preach. So began my ministry.

The following Sunday was the Harvest Festival and the preacher was the Bishop of Willesden, Gerald Ellison who I think at that time was one of the youngest Bishops in the Church of England. We were, of course, still in the days when Matins was the main service of the day. We had a full Church that morning. But that was the exception to the rule. In a working class parish like Kilburn we normally had a better attendance in the evening.

One of the grants I received for my financial support during ordination training came from the Church Pastoral Aid Society. As a grantee and also as serving in a parish supported by CPAS I had to sign on the dotted line that I would only take the Northward position at the Holy Table (the word 'altar' was frowned upon). This did not apply to me in my first year as deacon, but it meant that a priest was not allowed to celebrate Holy Communion from the Eastward position (facing the altar) which was more general in the rest of the Church. You had your back to the congregation whereas the evangelical minister stood at the side of the Table. This was in the days before the Westward position was introduced where you stand behind the Table and face the congregation. All this seems rather trivial and legalistic now and I think even CPAS have given up their insistence on the Northward position long ago. But in those days it mattered and showed where you stood doctrinally!

Raleigh Prater had only recently moved from Curate to Vicar in this parish. I was his guinea pig as I was the first Curate whom he trained. So it was a bit of trial and error. He was a good man and worked incredibly hard in this enormous parish. On his Staff were also two Church Army Sisters. They seemed to spend most of their time on women's meetings. There was – as I have already mentioned – the Women's Service. Quite a number of women came to it because they were not allowed by their husbands to go to Church on a Sunday. On other days of the week there was the Sunshine Circle (!), the Mothers' Union, the Guild of Womanhood (!) and the Ladies Home Mission Union (which was a branch of CPAS). Some of the women went to all of them in turn! In the summer all these meetings had their outings to the seaside. When they got there they first made a beeline to the nearest Woolworth's. The Staff were expected to go with them on all these outings which at least got us out of the parish.

We had a large Sunday School. It met in the afternoon as it had done since the Sunday School Movement began in the last century. Parents were very happy to send off their kids to Sunday School after lunch so that they could have a rest. Very few parents had cars which meant that they did not go out on Sundays. Once the car culture arrived it put an end to afternoon Sunday Schools. Quite naturally people wanted to get out of the stifling metropolis and enjoy the countryside or visit friends and relations. The arrival of the car altered the observance of the Sunday considerably. You can almost date the drop in Church attendance from that change.

We had some dedicated Sunday School teachers. Some of the children came from very poor homes and looked quite deprived. I remember one girl who came from a very difficult home. She later joined Church Army and became a Church Army Officer with several posts of considerable responsibility. One of many whose lives I saw transformed and redeemed by the grace of God. This is one of the joys and privileges that one has in the course of one's ministry. Before long, inevitably, I became Superintendent of the Sunday School and Jean was involved in it as well.

Nowadays Jean would have had a job to supplement our meagre stipend. As a nurse she would have had no difficulty finding some work. But very few clergy wives worked. They were expected to stay at home and often were the unpaid Curates. How we managed on £400 a year I don't know. Initially Jean's housekeeping money was two pounds ten shilling a week. Jean's father was able to give us £5 a month which made quite a difference. On our day off we made a point of getting out of the Parish. From our flat we could not see a single tree or any green spaces, just rows of terrace houses and high rise blocks of flats. I think it was the *Evening Standard* which produced 'Walks in the Countryside'. We used to catch the Green Line and go on some of these walks and then return for another week of fairly intensive work.

Quite soon I began to see the importance of visiting. In the mornings I was at Staff Meetings or preparing sermons or Sunday School material or did some further studying (The Diocese had a Post Ordination Course). In the afternoon whenever possible I was out and about in the parish. Sometimes Jean would come with me. I do think that there is something in the slogan 'a housegoing parson makes a Churchgoing people'. If your parishioners see that you are genuinely interested in their lives, that you share in their joys and sorrows, that you are there when they are in need, that you pray with them when they need God's help then they will often respond by coming to Church. You visit them for their sake, not in order to bring them into the Church. But it is a reciprocal relationship. The problem in a large parish like Kilburn was that there was never enough time to do all the visiting that was needed.

Before long the Vicar asked me to take on the leadership of the Young Communicants Guild (such a Victorian name would never do for young people fifty years later!). We had quite a number of young people and I threw myself into organising an interesting programme for them. It included outings and rambles and visiting other Youth Groups. Most Sunday afternoons we had some of our young people to tea before we all went off to the Evening Service. We suffered from the fact that as a downtown Church we could not compete with some of the thriving Churches further afield and we were disappointed when some of our keener members hived off to All Souls, Langham Place or Duke Street Baptist Church, Richmond.

There was also a Lads' Fellowship in the parish which catered for some of the boys from rough homes. It was run with great dedication by two of our lay men. They had an annual camp on the Isle of Wight. Jean and I were drafted in to help with the running of these camps. They were quite exhausting, but great fun.

My first Christmas will always stay in my memory. We had a daughter Church, St Jude's, with a very small congregation. At that time most churches still had an early Communion at 7 am at major festivals followed by another at 8 am. The 7 am was at St Jude's on that Christmas Day. I was there in good time, but my Vicar failed to turn up. I was still a deacon and could not celebrate. Sometime after 7 am the Churchwarden rang the Vicarage. The Vicar had overslept and was on his way. I started the service and fortunately the Vicar arrived in time to take over and celebrate the holy mysteries. Between the end of the 8 am Communion and the special Christmas Morning Service the Vicar always tried to fit in a visit to the local hospital. 11 am came, the Choir and I were lined up in the Vestry waiting for the Vicar. He had a habit of turning up for services at the last minute, but usually on time. This time again no sign of him. We could not keep the congregation waiting. We processed into a full Church. It was my first Christmas there and without the Vicar I felt somewhat nervous as he was due to preach the Christmas sermon. I took the first part of the service as planned, but still no sign of the preacher. I announced the hymn before the sermon. By now I was in a cold sweat. I had no sermon up my sleeve. During the last verse of the hymn the Vestry door opened and the Vicar went straight up into the pulpit. I breathed more than a sigh of relief! Cycling back from the hospital (it was some distance from the Church) he had a puncture and had to push the bicycle all the way back to the Church. I dread to think what would have happened if he had not got back in time for the sermon. I don't think at that stage I could have produced an impromptu message.

One of the great annual events in the parish was the Christmas Bazaar which was held in the Church Hall on a Thursday afternoon and all day Saturday. The women worked all the year round producing goods for the various stalls. The Vicar always had a special feature for the children (needless to say with Father Christmas) on the stage. I remember one year it was a replica of the seating area of an aeroplane which rocked to and fro and took children on imaginary flights. The Vicar spent hours and hours planning and constructing it, and always at the last minute. I and members of the Young Communicants' Guild were drafted in to help. We finished it in the early hours of the morning after several things had gone wrong. These special attractions were usually a great success, but took up an inordinate amount of time. The Bazaars made about £600 which in those days was a great deal of money. Considering that we were a rather poor parish it was quite remarkable.

Another event which took place during our time there was a Bible Lands Exhibition. It was organised by the Church's Mission to Jews with exhibits from the Holy Land, with talks and tableaux. A number of the congregation were involved, and had to be trained. They were dressed up in Eastern garments and illustrated some of the biblical scenes. It brought the Bible and the Holy Land to life. The other Churches in the area also supported it and brought their members along. It was hard work, but well worthwhile and it made quite an impression. One evening Asta, a young Jewish girl who had come over from Germany just before the war in a children's transport as a refugee walked into our Church Hall to look at the Exhibition. She was so impressed that she came back the next evening. We got to know her and befriended her. At the end of the week she had become a radiant Christian. Later she joined Church Army and became a Sister and worked in some of their homes. Eventually she got married. We are still in touch with her.

Two evangelistic events took place while we were at Kilburn. We had a Parish Mission with teams of students from the London College of Divinity and the CMS Training Colleges at Chislehurst. Having recently come from LCD and been involved in several College Missions I probably suggested it in the first place. It was quite an ambitious undertaking to have a

Mission in the parish. It meant accommodating something like thirty folk. Not many of our congregation were used to putting visitors up nor did many of them have a spare room. We had a number of preliminary meetings to plan the Mission. We prepared the congregation and publicised it around the parish. There were the usual Mission Services in the evenings and on the two Sundays. There were visits to schools, house meetings, visits to the various Church organisations. We held several Open Air Meetings. The corner of St Luke's Church which used to be the main Church in the parish and was still a ruin after it had been bombed in the war provided a good venue for these meetings. It was near Queen's Park Underground Station and on the main road.

The theme of the Mission was 'Christ is the Key' and posters with this slogan could be seen all over the parish. As a result of the Mission a number of new people came into the Church. But apart from numbers it was a great spiritual experience for those who took part and also for the congregation. It focussed our minds on the Good News of Jesus Christ and it put the Church on the map.

However, this Mission was soon followed and surpassed by the first Billy Graham Mission at Harringay. This was something on a scale which had never been attempted before. It was on an ambitious American scale. And there was inevitably a great deal of controversy beforehand. Was it a gimmick? Why did we need to import an American evangelist? Would it be a terrible flop? I remember being invited with hundreds of other clergy to a breakfast at the Cafe Royal at Piccadilly to meet and hear Billy Graham. I was impressed with his sincerity and conviction. He spoke with authority reminiscent of the one he came to proclaim. Soon all over London groups were set up to train people as counsellors, stewards, choir. It was all extremely well organised. I joined a counselling class where we had to learn key verses from the Bible off by heart. It was all a bit juvenile, but it provided a framework for some people. And it was all part of an enormous build-up towards the Crusade.

The day came when it began. By this time there were posters on buses, in tube stations, on hoardings. For the first time people in the street talked about this strange religious phenomenon. It was quite exciting. Religion was news! For the first two or three days the big arena at Harringay was not quite full and some doubting Thomases wondered whether it was going to peter out. But after the third day all the critics were proved wrong. Night after night the place was full and the Crusade had to be extended into July.

We used to take coachloads from Kilburn and again, as in the days of the great missionary rallies, it was thrilling to see thousands converging on Harringay. It was a moving experience to see people coming out of their seats and making their way to the front of the Hall to respond to the call for a decision for Christ. In a way it was quite uncanny for there was nothing new in the message, but in this setting it made a much bigger impact than back in the local Church. It was equally moving to be a counsellor and talk to some of these 'enquirers' after Dr Graham had had another word with them up at the front. Of course, not all of them were there and then converted. Many were Christians and members of various Churches. The Crusade gave them the opportunity to renew their faith. Others slipped through the net between Harringay and linking them with a local Church. Sadly, many local Churches could not live up to the expectations of these enquirers and they drifted away again. But nevertheless, some were brought into the fellowship of the Church and I know of a number of clergy who can trace back their call to the ministry to one of the Billy Graham Crusades. Years later we heard him again when he came to Ibadan, but there one was aware that he came with his American trappings and had not attuned himself to the African culture.

One interesting change was noticeable in Kilburn towards the end of our time there. Most of the Victorian houses near the Church were now divided up into flats. Here and there West Indian families would move into one or other of these three storey houses. The people below or above them would begin to complain about the noise and the cooking smells. In due course, these people would move out and make room for another West Indian family. It was the beginning of the Caribbean immigration. It was brought about in the first place by London Transport who advertised in the West Indies for staff. When you go to Kilburn today you will find that almost every other person you pass in the street is black or coloured.

Since the fifties Britain, or at least its big cities, have become quite a different society. We are now a multi-racial society. Some people might regret this development. Others would say that the presence of other races and cultures in our midst has enriched the life of our society. It has certainly altered the missionary approach. No longer are peoples of other faiths thousands of miles away. They are in our midst and in many cases on our doorstep. There are now more Muslims than Methodists in this country. It all began in the early fifties when we were in Kilburn.

Looking back on my three years at Kilburn I learnt an enormous amount during that first Curacy. I learnt from the dedicated leadership of a faithful man like Raleigh Prater. I learnt from the tough environment of a working class area. I learnt from the simple faith of many ordinary Christians in the Church there. It was a tough, but good training place for the future. But by today's standards the Church was still remarkably traditional. The worship was based on the Book of Common Prayer. There was nothing else and one took it for granted that this was the only valid liturgy for the Church of England. One looked up to one's elders. Bishops belonged to a higher realm and one stood in awe of them. Even our Rural Dean, Prebendary Oscar Hardman, seemed a venerable gentleman whom one would never address by his Christian name. We had good relations with our Methodist neighbours, but none with the Roman Catholics. If you passed their priest in the street you might just politely nod your head, but would never speak to him.

The Church in general was well staffed and well established. There was a constant stream of ordinands despite the poor pay that the Church offered. Most rural villages still had their own clergy and you went to a country parish for your last living prior to retirement. These were the relatively gentle days before the storm when suddenly in the early sixties the permissive society began and in the Church liturgical reform, the 'Honest to God' debate and Vatican II. I wonder whether the Church as I knew it in the first half of the fifties was prepared for these convulsions.

In 1955 my three years as Curate were up and it was time to look for a second Curacy. We went to see one or two parishes.

I remember going to Barnet in North London to look at a parish which was quite promising. But God had other plans for us. My father knew Max Warren, the General Secretary of the Church Missionary Society, from his Cambridge days. Partly through this family link, but also through the missionary stimulus which I had received at LCD I had taken quite an interest in the work of CMS. During our Parish Mission I had met quite a number of recruits from the CMS Training College. Jean, on her part, through her membership in the London Inter Varsity Christian Union had also brought into our marriage a keen interest in the Church overseas. One day while we were considering second curacies we went to tea with Graeme Spiers, my best man who was then Curate at Addiscombe. He told us that he was thinking of offering for service overseas. On the way home we said to each other – if Graeme is thinking of it there is no reason why we should not think of it either. We made a phone call to CMS to make preliminary enquiries and that more or less settled out future for the next eight years! From that moment our lives were taken in a different direction.

# 11

# CMS Training and Teaching in Nigeria (1955–1963)

WE were summoned to CMS to have the usual interviews. I remember being shown into the big Boardroom at Salisbury Square (where CMS had its headquarters before it moved to a tailor made new building in Waterloo Road) and being confronted by a rather intimidating Candidates' Committee. We had our medicals. And before we knew where we were we were accepted for training at Liskeard Lodge, Chislehurst. With a heavy heart we said goodbye to the parish at Kilburn. We had made many friends among old and young. We had even grown to love our little flat among its depressing surroundings. For the next year our accommodation was reduced to one room.

We found that when our training began in September 1955 Liskeard Lodge was over-subscribed. It was bursting at the seams with new recruits. There was no room for us. With three other couples we were farmed out to St Julians in Coolham, Sussex. We knew St Julians already. It had come into being after the war as a venture by a former CMS missionary, Florence Allshorn. It was to be a rest house mainly for missionaries on furlough, but also for clergy and other Churchworkers who needed a break. It is run by a small community of ladies who in the past had been missionaries themselves. The comfortable house is set in lovely grounds with a lake and looking out on the Downs. There is also a beautiful Chapel with straw on the floor. You start the day with breakfast in bed which is brought to you by a member of the community. It is all very conducive to a rest in a loving Christian atmosphere. Since 1952 we had been there several times for short breaks from the parish. And here we began our missionary training, with breakfast in bed which must be pretty unique!

That treat actually only lasted a few days. Then I think,
unlike the other guests in the house, we got up for breakfast.
Margaret Potts, who was the leader of the Community at that
time, gave us a few lectures. Otherwise we studied on our own
in their extensive Library or worked in the garden. It was a
very gentle introduction to being a missionary. It only lasted a
few weeks. At half term we said goodbye to St Julians. CMS
had found us overflow accommodation at Maxwell House, a
Children's Home belonging to the China Inland Mission (now
the Overseas Missionary Fellowship) which was just the other
side of the Common in Chislehurst. It meant that we just had
to walk or cycle across the Common to Liskeard Lodge and
could take our full part in the training there.

There were two Training Colleges, both at Chislehurst. One
was for the men and married couples at Liskeard Lodge, and
the other for the women in a much nicer setting and in a
gracious mansion at Foxbury. This was just a walk down the
road from Liskeard Lodge. Most of the time the two communities functioned separately, but we joined forces for some of the
lectures. Douglas Sargent was the Principal of the Men's
College. He and Imogen, his vivacious American wife, had
been missionaries in China. From Chislehurst he went a few
years later to York as bishop of Selby. The Vice-Principal was
Wilfred Brown. He and Joan, his wife, had worked in India.
We shall hear of him later in a different context. They were a
good team, Douglas giving very able leadership and Wilfred
providing learning and wisdom.

CMS placed great importance on the training of their missionaries. It was assumed that the period of training would be
at least a year unless there were some exceptional circumstances. And that was for clergy and laity alike. It might be
asked why it was necessary to insist on this period of training
before going overseas. Clergy in particular had their spiritual
formation at theological College and that should have been
sufficient preparation for work abroad. A year's further preparation at home seemed rather a luxury. But the transition to a
different climate and culture and civilisation means an enormous adjustment which one can only realise when one is
immersed in it. I shall always be glad that we were given this
gradual adjustment from West to East. No doubt, we made

enough mistakes and blunders when we were in Africa. We would have made many more had we not been prepared for the culture shock of another continent.

We did a great deal of study and reading in training, but the academic approach was not the one that mattered most. CMS placed great stress on the importance of relationships. They owed much to the influence of Florence Allshorn who brought St Julians into being. She had been a young missionary in East Africa and before long had experienced a complete breakdown of communication with her senior missionary on the 'station'. Every missionary society will bear testimony to the sad fact that some of their recruits have to come home prematurely, sometimes even during their first tour because of culture shock or strained relationships with fellow missionaries or nationals. This, needless to say, seriously impairs the Christian witness. Florence Allshorn as a result of her experience laid great stress on learning to live in community.

That was also the primary ethos of the CMS Training Colleges. When you live in close proximity with families and single men, often from very different backgrounds, people who even as Christians you do not always find congenial and might not choose as fellow-workers then you are bound to get some of your corners knocked off in the course of a whole year. We were clergy, teachers, doctors, agriculturalists, technicians, all sharing in equal measure this life in community. I had my apprehensions before we went into training. I liked my privacy and independence. I wondered how I would cope in a community where I would be exposed to the intrusions of other members. But although we had our moments it turned out to be a most valuable year. It was not always easy and there were clashes of personalities and problems of accepting each other. But it was a very good test of Christian humility and forgiveness and acceptance. And on the positive side community provides mutual support and a deep experience of Christian fellowship. And when the training is geared not towards a Church that one is familiar with, but towards new communities in very different cultures and environments it assumes an extra dimension. We were trying all the time to begin the process of relating to Church and Mission in Africa and Asia.

We had regular visits from Secretaries of CMS who had

recently been overseas and reported to us on their trips and
kept us informed on the news of the 'younger' Churches (as
they were still called then). We were particularly blessed to
have occasional visits and lectures by Max Warren, the General
Secretary of the Society. He was the outstanding missionary
statesman of his time not only in the Anglican Communion,
but in the world Church. He particularly enjoyed meeting with
us clergy to thrash out some current theological issues on the
Mission of the Church. You could hear in his voice the
excitement about the work that he was engaged in. He died in
1977 after he had retired from being Sub-Dean of Westminster
Abbey. This is how one of the obituaries assesses his influence:

> As general secretary of the Church Missionary Society for 21
> years Max Warren exercised great leadership and by his writing
> even more than his speaking he held a wide influence. In many
> respects he was a prophet. He saw clearly the change in relation-
> ships which would become necessary between Church and Mis-
> sion in the aftermath of the Second World War and he did as
> much as anyone to prepare church people in Europe and America
> for the various revolutions, political, social, economic and educa-
> tional that were to have their way in Asia and Africa. He is
> believed to have refused the offer of more than one bishopric
> during his career, saying that he felt he could contribute more
> usefully to the Church the work he was doing at CMS.

Back at College we worked and worshipped and played together. One afternoon a week we were all out in the large
garden, hoeing and digging and planting. One evening a week
was a Fellowship Evening when we brought our mending or
hobbies and listened to letters from missionaries in various
parts of the world. On Sundays we were busy with deputations
or attended local Churches. Chislehurst was a very convenient
base. It was easy to get up to town. It was also well placed to
get out into the Kentish countryside.

For us personally it was an important year. Jean was expect-
ing our first child while we were in training. As we approached
the end of our year's training the big question in all our minds
was where we were going to be sent. It seemed fairly clear
early on that I was likely to be involved in some kind of
theological training. We gathered from one of the interviews
which we had that it was probably going to be in East Africa.

*Missionary training 1955*

*On way to a lecture, Immanuel College, Ibadan 1960*

*With a student at Immanuel College, Ibadan*

We were quite looking forward to that. How great was our surprise when we were told that we would be located to the other side of Africa, i.e. Nigeria. Sometime in June we were formally accepted as missionaries. After a final service of commissioning we dispersed to serve in the Churches of Asia and Africa and the Middle East.

This was still the time when missionary work was in its heyday. I think at that time CMS had over 1,000 missionaries in the field. In Afria CMS had quite strong contingents in Nigeria, Uganda, Kenya, Tanzania. There were no restrictions in sending missionaries. But at least we had now reached the point where they had to be formally requested and invited by the Churches overseas.

Our departure to Nigeria was delayed because Ruth was born in July 1956 and it was considered wiser to wait a few months before we took her out to the tropics. However, we knew that we were going to Melville Hall, the Anglican theological College in Ibadan. I have in front of me a flattering letter from Max Warren. He had sent me a copy of a series of essays edited by him entitled *The Triumph of God*. A number of (in those days well known) missionary and theological writers has contributed to it. In the letter Max says:

> I cannot tell you how delighted I am to know that you are going to Ibadan and the theological College there. These are days when the Church of Nigeria is so preoccupied with enjoying its independence and wrestling with administrative problems and sharing in the political effervescence of the times that it is in real danger of forgetting the spiritual realities. Melville Hall, Ibadan is a key institution and it needs the best we can put into it.

We spent the autumn at the Vicarage in Hampstead where my father was now Vicar of St Luke's (he went there at the age of 65 when most clergy nowadays retire!). We used the time to equip ourselves, had our inoculations, enjoyed our first baby and celebrated Christmas with our two sets of parents. On one of the last days of 1956 we embarked on the *Auriol* at Liverpool and sailed for Nigeria. The ship belonged to the Elder Dempster Line which does not exist anymore.

There were two classes on the boat – First Class and Cabin Class. As missionaries we travelled Cabin Class and were in the bowels of the boat. A number of other missionaries were sailing with us. It was my first experience of being on the high seas. We soon ran into rough weather in the Bay of Biscay and I found to my dismay that I was not a good sailor. It would not have mattered, but I was the only clergyman on board and was asked to take the early Sunday morning Communion. I dreaded it as the boat was heaving and I only just managed to survive without disgracing myself. Once we were past Gibraltar we came into calmer conditions and before long we were under blue skies and in brilliant sunshine.

We called briefly at Bathurst (which today is Banjul in Gambia) where the Bishop of Gambia came on board. But our first proper experience of Africa – eagerly anticipated – was when we docked at Freetown. Lots of little wooden canoes greeted us and surrounded our boat. The youngsters in those little boats dived for coins which passengers threw down to them. Cecil Horstead, the Bishop of Sierra Leone, was also at that time Archbishop of West Africa. He met us off the boat and took us in his car up to Bishopscourt. The drive through Freetown was our first introduction to the heat, the smells, the sounds and the sights of Africa. After lunch on the verandah of Bishopscourt the Archbishop drove us up to Fourah Bay College, the oldest West African educational establishment. We also stopped off briefly at Freetown Cathedral which is full of memorial tablets to missionaries who only months or even weeks after their arrival had succumbed to malaria and other tropical diseases. Here one was vividly reminded of the meaning of 'white man's grave' which was true of so many who came to West Africa with the Gospel in the last century. After this first introduction to Africa we returned to the boat to resume our voyage via Takoradi on the Gold Coast (now Ghana) to Lagos.

Those last few days along the coast were extremely trying. The heat, especially in our cabin with no air-conditioning, was almost unbearable. I paced the deck at 6 am just to get some fresh air. It was a great relief when we arrived at Apapa, the port of Lagos. After rather slow formalities to get our luggage and crates through customs we were whisked off to the CMS Guest House on the Marina next door to the large Victorian Cathedral. The Guest House was then an old wooden structure going back to the last century. It has since been rebuilt, but is still in the same prime position. We were met by David Anderson, who with his family had preceded us to Melville Hall as Principal of the College. Previously he had been on the staff of St Aidan's Birkenhead, a theological College in the North which disappeared long ago. CMS were very fortunate in having recruited David. He brought to the College gifts of leadership and theological expertise.

In 1957 Nigeria was still a British Colony under a Governor General and regional Governors, all British. This, however, was soon to change. Nigeria is one of the biggest countries in Africa with a population of 50–60 million people according to the statistics then. Today the figure is nearer 100 million. The Church was already largely indigenised. A number of the Bishops were Nigerians and so were most of the parochial clergy. But there were still a considerable number of missionaries, mainly from Britain and the United States. Alone in the CMS Yoruba Mission in the West of the country there must have been about thirty or more missionaries with a full-time Mission Secretary, George Vellacott, who was based in Lagos and was also at the CMS Guest House to welcome us when we arrived.

We spent the first night under mosquito nets and tossed and turned in the humid air that enveloped us from now on. Life starts early in Africa, long before dawn, and we woke to all the strange new sounds from a busy city. Later that morning David Anderson took us up to Ibadan in his car. First through the busy streets of Lagos with its wayside stalls, women gracefully carrying their loads on their heads, carhorns hooting, traders offering their wares. A colourful scene which soon became part and parcel of our everyday life. Once we were on the open road David speeded up – he was a very fast, but safe driver – and gave us some anxious moments. For we soon discovered that Africans are not such safe drivers. The road between Lagos and Ibadan, about 100 miles' distance, was very busy. Like most African roads it was only one width. You had to get off the tarmac to avoid oncoming traffic. When you came round bends or approached a bridge you would find that the car or lorry coming towards you did not make room for you to pass. Nor would they have been able to slow down because in many cases their brakes were not very reliable. We got to know this road very well and one of the topics of conversation when you had safely negotiated it was 'How many wrecks did you see today?' Eventually we reached the outskirts of Ibadan. It was a great moment when we finally arrived at our destination which was going to be our home for the next seven years.

In January 1853 David and Anna Hinderer whom CMS had recruited from Germany landed in Badagry (not far from Lagos) and slowly made their way via Abeokuta to Ibadan. Even then Ibadan was the largest African town in Africa with well over 100,000 people. Now it is fast becoming a mega city with several million inhabitants. The Hinderers were the first white people to enter Ibadan. In the *Swelling of Jordan*, a book which records their trials and tribulations there is a wonderful story of their approach to the city. 'They dismount from their horses and kneel for a prayer "Lord, we have come at last to this stronghold of Sin and Satan (!). With thy help, O Lord of Hosts, we shall attack and take it." David thinks that they should make themselves as neat as possible before entering the town. Anna changes her travelling dress for a more formal one and dons her best bonnet and shawl. He puts his Sunday best on and puts his black 'stove-pipe' hat on. There is a discussion among them whether he should carry a Bible under his arm when he rides into the town. But they decide against it because he wants to keep his arm free to salute people.' And so in 1853 the Hinderers establish a Christian Mission at Kudeti on the outskirts of the town.

Years later on one of our leaves I went round the new Anglican Cathedral in Liverpool. On one of the staircases I discovered a stained glass window in memory of the Hinderers. They would be delighted now if they revisited Ibadan. In what had been an entirely pagan town 100 years earlier there are now a number of thriving Churches of all denominations and of many African sects as well. Ibadan is probably now half Christian and half Muslim. Melville Hall, the theological College, was situated just one hundred yards from the first CMS 'Station' in Kudeti. On the site stands now St David's Church, named after David Hinderer.

On the compound were three staff houses. The Andersons were in the Principal's house. We moved into the next one and on our other side were the Foulkes. Francis had been a Rhodes scholar. He and his family came from New Zealand. He had worked under the previous warden and was already quite fluent in Yoruba. Our bungalow was quite simple – a main living room where we had our meals, and two rooms on either side one of which became my study and the other was our bedroom. Ruth was about six months when we arrived in Ibadan. Behind the living room was the kitchen and a store room. When we moved in there was just the minimum of furniture in the house. Gradually the College carpenter added a few more items to it. Apart from the staff houses there were a few wooden huts left over from previous occupants of this site. They served as lecture rooms, library and office, Chapel, and dormitories for the students which again were extremely basic. Soon after our arrival Francis took us to 'greet' Bishop Akinyele who had been Bishop of Ibadan and was now a very old man. He was the immediate descendent of one of the first converts in Ibadan and so a direct link with the beginning of the Church in this big city.

Term started soon after our arrival and I was thrown in at the deep end. We had 56 students that year. Most of them had been teachers or catechists, mainly from Western Nigeria. They came from different language areas, so the common language was English. Soon after our arrival one of the students (who later became a Bishop) tried to teach me Yoruba. As the only time available for it was in the heat of the afternoon I did not make much progress. It is a very difficult language with three tones (high, middle and low). I still regret that I never mastered the language beyond the customary greetings of which there are many for every conceivable occasion. I was asked to lecture on the Old Testament which became my special subject during the whole time. Apparently the students called me 'Mr OT'. I was delighted that I could make it my own because the Old Testament is so closely related to the African way of life. It is interesting that the Christian names of most Nigerian Christians are taken from the Old Testament. In practice, it was hardly possible to specialise. Sooner or later one or other of the European Staff would go on leave and one had to stand in and teach their subject as well. Unless the text books were very simple the students did very little reading, they relied heavily on the notes which they took during lectures and then very often regurgitated them in exams at the end of term or end of the year.

A common saying among them was that 'the pew is higher than the pulpit'. It expressed their justified apprehension that in many churches there were now laity in the pews who were intellectually superior to the clergy. We were also aware of this trend and tried very hard over the next few years to upgrade the academic standard. We introduced a Diploma in Theology and even a London B.D. It was only towards the end of our time that slowly more candidates emerged who academically could measure up to the lawyers and teachers and businessmen whom one would find especially in urban congregations.

The College had no administrative staff. The Foulkes were going on leave soon after we arrived and within my first term Francis Foulkes handed over to me the job of College Bursar. It meant keeping the books and dealing with the students' financial transactions. It was quite a time consuming job and sometimes I used to spend hours and hours on a Saturday trying to balance the books at the end of the week.

The worship in the churches was by and large traditional Book of Common Prayer. The hymns, too, came straight from 'Ancient and Modern'. To listen to the dreary singing of our Western hymns was quite depressing. They just did not go with the African temperament. But it was quite a different sound when they sang Yoruba hymns. The men suddenly came to life and began to sway to their inimitable rhythm. We tried to introduce in our Chapel Services the use of drums and other indigenous instruments in the hope that the students would encourage the use of native music back in their local churches. But generally speaking there was a tendency to ape our Western pattern. When the students approached their ordination they used to send off their orders for robes and other ecclesiastical garments to Wippells and would spend hundreds of pounds which they could barely afford. It used to grieve us, especially when local tailors were quite able to copy designs at ridiculously cheap prices. But no amount of argument would persuade our men to patronise the local trade. It had to be the real thing and have the genuine label.

Apart from these needlessly expensive obsessions the students were with few exceptions a delightful body of men both in our endeavour to train them and also in the more informal contacts. Most of them had left their families behind and never saw them in term time. They were all hard up and often had to be supported by their extended families. Many of them became faithful pastors. Alone of the final year when we arrived several are now bishops and a number of other from subsequent years have become bishops and archdeacons.

Once a year the students went on what was called an 'itineration' or what we would call a mission. It was an opportunity for them to apply what they had learnt in the classroom and to evangelise. I remember going with David Anderson to a very remote area in the creeks where one pastor looked after a large number of Churches. How we ever got there I can't think. The roads were atrocious. Several times the car got stuck in the deep ruts and had to be dug out. Some of the villages could only be reached by canoe. In some of the places we visited the local people stared at us because they had never seen a white face. It was a valuable experience not only for the students, but also for us. The church in the bush was very different from the churches we knew in Ibadan. Our day used to start before dawn, at about 5 am when we would meet in the dimly lit church for morning prayers. After that the villagers would go out to their farms. In the evenings I would show slides on my projector which operated from David Anderson's car battery. We felt like some of the early pioneer missionaries.

All our bishops in the Yoruba Region, i.e. Western Nigeria, were now Nigerians. The Bishop of Ibadan, Odutola, was a strong leader. I had a high regard for him. He was the Chairman of the College Council for a number of years and I got to know him well. During the time I was there Bishop Howells of Lagos, another Nigerian, died. I went down to Lagos on behalf of the College to express my condolence. I was ushered into a large room at Bishopscourt where a number of mourners sat in a circle. Hardly a word was spoken. People came and went. I sat in this circle for about an hour and then departed again. It reminded me very much of Job's three friends who sat with Job for seven days and seven nights in complete silence. I found it a very moving experience. That hour sitting where the mourners sat spoke more strongly than any amount of words or sympathy. All the parochial clergy were Nigerians. Missionaries were still found in theological education, in some of the Teacher Training Colleges, Secondary Schools, as Bishops' Chaplains and one or two other specialist posts. We all came together for the annual Mission Conference. The CMS folk in Ibadan used to meet regularly for Bible study and prayer. There were, of course, many other expatriates in Lagos and Ibadan and all over the country. Among them we enjoyed meeting many fine Christians who worked at the University, the Hospitals, the Colleges of Education. Today the situation is quite different. The number of missionaries and expatriates has shrunk considerably. In the Sixties and Seventies there was a drive by the government to 'nigerianise' the professions and the business world.

Our relations with our Nigerian colleagues were on the whole good, although looking back on it now I realise that I probably should have been even more sensitive and discerning. On the surface they were polite, but I wonder whether they sometimes got rather incensed with our Western ways. I hope we no longer gave them the impression of appearing superior. Socially it was difficult to mix. This was partly because Yoruba food is very spicey and our palate finds it hard to cope with it, partly because in general a meal is for them not a social occasion. We used to invite two or three students at a time for tea. That was probably an ordeal for them. They often preferred just to drop in for no apparent reason. They would look at a magazine or at our photo-album (a very favourite custom) and then depart again. Infant mortality was still very high, often due to malaria or poor feeding habits. Many of our students lost children. They would come to tell you and just shrug their shoulders. It was a way of life that they had become accustomed to.

We had some links with the Religious Studies Department at the University. Geoffrey Parrinder later became Professor at King's College, London. Maurice Wiles was later Regius Professor at Oxford and for a time headed up the Doctrine Commission of the Church of England. Simon Barrington-Ward was then a Junior member of the Department. Jean Taylor was a doctor at the University and looked after the health of all

CMS missionaries in Ibadan. We watched the romance between her and Simon which blossomed into marriage. Simon later succeeded me as Principal of the CMS Training College when it moved up to Selly Oak. Then he became General Secretary of CMS and now he is the Bishop of Coventry. A small contingent of Methodist students also trained for the ministry in Ibadan. They were in a different part of the town, but used to come over for some of the lectures. David Anderson's brief was to merge the two institutions and form a Union College. This actually took place only a year after our arrival. Melville Hall became Immanuel College with students from both denominations living and training on our site. This meant building two more Staff houses for Methodist tutors and also accommodation for the extra students.

On St Valentine' Day 1958 the united College was inaugurated at a solemn Service at St David's Church in the presence of the regional Governor, the Oba (king) of Ibadan, representatives from the University and the Bishop of Ibadan as well as the Methodist Chairman. It was a great occasion. With the arrival of the Methodist students we now had 66 men and soon two new Methodist members of Staff with their families on the compound. There is no doubt that the coming together of the two traditions was a great enrichment of our common life. We shared fully in each other's worship and sacramental life. I don't recall that it caused any difficulties. In fact, very quickly the student body was so well integrated that we found it hard to remember who was Anglican and who was Methodist. Ever since those days I have considered myself half a Methodist and have enjoyed sharing in their worship and fellowship whenever the opportunity arose.

One of the highlights of our time in Nigeria was the first All Africa Church Conference which took place in Ibadan and was held at the Anglican Girls' School quite close to us. Well over a hundred delegates from all over Africa came together, including a few from South Africa. Some of the leaders of the World Church and the missionary movement were there. Bishop Stephen Neill visited the College. Some of our students acted as stewards at the Conference and caught a glimpse of the wider Church. At the final Communion Service they ran out of bread and they could not hold up the service to find

some more. Canon Banjo who had organised the service de-
vised this form of words for those who had to go without it
'Believe that thou has eaten'!

We had a constant stream of visitors who came up from
Lagos and would call in at the College. Max Warren stayed
and was particularly interested in the new Union College. John
V. Taylor when he was Africa Secretary of CMS visited the
College more than once and so did Douglas Webster, my
former tutor at LCD when he was Theologian Missioner at
CMS. In fact, we used to say that we saw far more visitors
there than we would ever have met at home. American visitors
who made a brief stop and did the whole country in three
weeks and then wrote a book on Nigeria were not particularly
welcome! But one of our surprise visitors one afternoon was
Dr Coggan. A car drove into the compound and he stepped
out. Fortunately we were in and were delighted. He was then
Bishop of Bradford and was on a brief visit to the country.

The Christian Council of Nigeria comprised all the main
Christian Churches except the Romans. For a time I was
Secretary of one of their sub-Committees. In that capacity I
went as one of the delegates to their big Conference in Calabar
right on the other side of Nigeria. It was chaired by Sir Francis
Ibiam, one of the great Nigerian Christian laymen. It was in
Calabar that one of the first Christian Missions began. The
grave of Mary Slessor is there.

That trip was my first opportunity to see the East or the
Iboland. On the way back we stopped off in Onitsha and saw
the beautiful new Anglican Cathedral there. It was still in the
making and was only completed quite recently. I visited the
East again a year or two later when I was asked to give the
Bible Readings at a Clergy School. There I met for the first
time Bishop Cecil Patterson who later became Archbishop of
Nigeria. He was a saintly man and suffered greatly in spirit
later during the Biafran war. I saw more of him towards the
end of his life when he lived in Richmond. It always felt good
to be in his company. During that visit I saw most of the East
including the Oji River Leper Settlement where CMS did a
wonderful work.

Another time-consuming job came my way. The Church in
the West had a magazine which had been running for many

years and was called *In Leisure Hours*. It was a strange title for a Church publication. It had a circulation of about 5,000 and included daily Bible Readings in Yoruba produced by the Scripture Union. The magazine came out monthly. There was a crisis of editorship and it was a question of either closing it down or for us at Immanuel College to take it on and edit it. I used to spend hours pasting up the various contributions, persuading people to write articles, taking it to the printers and, worst of all, keeping to a deadline. It was a useful experience in publishing, but it took up far too much time alongside my other teaching commitments in the College. It meant even less leisure hours for me and less time with the family.

While we were in Nigeria our other two children were born. Both were baptised in the College Chapel, one by David Anderson, the other by Archdeacon Jadesimi. The African custom of naming the child is almost as important as the christening. The wider family participates in the names given to the child. I remember struggling through some seven or more Yoruba or Ibo names when I baptised Nigerian babies in Kilburn. The students of Immanuel College were our extended family in Nigeria and so the elders of the students added their Yoruba names. Hilary Joy was also named Ayo (which means joy) and David Andrew was given the names Bamidele Olu-wole. They mean 'child born far from home' and 'head of the home' because he was a boy. Whenever we drove out of the compound with the children the local kids would call out 'Oyinbo'. This is the word for European, but literally means 'peeled'. According to African traditions we were all born brown or black, but we Europeans peeled off the outer layer of skin and underneath was the white skin.

Two of our local leaves were spent in the North of Nigeria. This was partly in order to get away from the stifling humility in the South and to have the relief of some cooler nights. This was possible on the plateau up in the North. Once we flew to Jos and had a holiday at Miango, the rest place of the Sudan Interior Mission (SIM) which was mainly American.

As an Anglican I was first viewed with some reserve, but when they found that I was sound in the faith I was allowed to say grace at mealtime. And their graces were not just one sentence! For our second leave in the North we drove up in our little car. By then we had acquired a Morris Minor Traveller thanks to a compensation by the German government for victims of Nazism. We stopped off in Bida and saw the Fulanis. They are a tribe of rather beautiful cattle people. We just happened to see one of their initiation rites. The young men are beaten with sticks and must not show any sign of pain. The young girls hold up mirrors into their faces so that they can make sure that they don't flinch. This time we stayed at the agricultural resthouse at Vom. Just to sleep one night without waking up in a pool of sweat was a great treat.

Roughly every eighteen months we went on home leave. Part of each leave was taken up with deputations to Link Churches, i.e. Churches who had adopted us and supported us with their prayers and in other practical ways. On one of our leaves I did some Old Testament study with Professor Ulrich Simon at King's College. The best leave was in the autumn of 1960 when we had the use of Margaret Potts' Cottage at Coolham. This meant that we were close to St Julians and could also use their library. It was good to enjoy the seasons at home. In Nigeria there was just the difference between the dry and the wet season.

Unfortunately, because of that leave we missed the Independence celebrations in Nigeria. In October 1960 the country attained its independence. It became a Federation mainly of the three large language areas – Hausa (North), Yoruba (West) and Ibo (East). Their first Head of State was Sir Abubakar Tafawa Balewa, a cultured and dignified Northerner. Under his leadership there were great hopes and expectations for the future of the country. We felt proud to work in this great new nation. Sadly, before long these hopes were cruelly shattered.

Independence brought a greater self-awareness and autonomy. The changes were also felt in the College. Two very promising young clergy came back from UK with degrees and soon made their mark as members of Staff – Joseph Adetiloye and Gideon Olajide. The former is now Archbishop of Nigeria and Bishop of Lagos, the latter Bishop of Ibadan.

In 1962 David Anderson was appointed Principal of Wycliffe Hall, Oxford and left the College in August to take up his new appointment. His departure was a great loss to us personally as well as to the College. David has been a very good 'boss' and our two families were almost inseparable. Their children were roughly the same age as our three and they played together every day. Helen Anderson is Hilary's godmother and I am Jeremy's godfather. But their departure affected us also directly in another way. It was a logical step that the next Principal should be a Nigerian. The obvious choice was Revd A. Adegbola, an outstanding Methodist minister who was running a Lay Training Centre. However, he was not available till 1963. In the meantime I was asked to be acting Principal. We decided to take a short leave of two months during the long summer vacation. David was born on 25th June. A fortnight later we flew home. David was then one of the youngest babies they had ever carried on this plane. When we returned in September the Andersons had left and I held the fort until Adegbola arrived in March 1963.

Ever since the College became a united institution it was hoped that one day it would move nearer to the University and establish a special relationship with it. At the end of 1961 the State had offered us a splendid site of 68 acres right next door to the University at a peppercorn rent of 1 shilling a year. Now it was a question of raising the funds for the rebuilding of the College on that site. There were the inevitable delays with architects, builders and finance. Eventually on 2nd July 1963 the First Sod was turned on the new site and building began in earnest.

By then Adegbola had arrived as the new Principal and we had decided that the time had come for us to return to the UK. Ruth was now seven years old. The only suitable school for her was the Staff School at the University which was right at the other end of the town, several miles away. It was also time that she and the other two children got settled at home. Little children thrive in the tropical climate, but when they got to about 8 they tend to become rather pale and thin. They need the more bracing air of our island. We also felt that we had made our contribution to the Church in Nigeria. With a Nigerian Principal a new dispensation had begun and the move to the new site seemed the right moment for us to leave. Politically the strain of the three very different parts of the young Federation began to tell. There were clashes between the political parties. The (Nigerian) Governor of the West was assassinated. A State of Emergency was declared. The school run to the University became more difficult because of roadblocks manned by the army. There were also frequent roadblocks on the main roads to Lagos and upcountry which caused long hold-ups and could be quite unpleasant. It was sad to see this promising nation slowly descending into chaos and civil war. Soon after we left the Biafran War began.

The students staged a farewell football match for us at which I had to perform the kick-off and on 9th November 1963 after nearly seven years in Ibadan we boarded the boat that took us back to England. The following year the College opened on the new site near the University. I felt like Moses who saw the promised land from afar, but never entered it. Fortunately over twenty years later I had the opportunity to go back to Nigeria. I returned to Ibadan and visited Immanuel College. It was a great thrill after all that time to see what we had planned and prayed for.

I am profoundly grateful to God that he called us to serve in the Church in Africa and that we had the opportunity of living and working on that Continent. Africa is constantly in the news and is still in the process, through many tribulations, to come into its own. I remember the Africa Correspondent of *The Times* saying to us in the Sixties that it would take at least 40 years for the new nations of Africa to be firmly established. The present evidence is that it will take more than forty years. Having lived there and experienced at close quarters the aspirations and frustrations of one nation on that Continent I think that I am in a better position to understand their problems and convulsions. Every time there is a documentary or news report from some part of Africa and I hear the familiar sounds and see the sights it brings back so many vivid memories.

On the whole Africans are very happy people. They are much more relaxed than we are. Their concept of time is very different from ours. We are so bound by time, for them it is a much more flexible commodity. Sometimes one would go to Church and find that the service had already started before time because people had turned up early. At other times one would wait and wonder whether the service would start at all. And nobody minded if the service went on for a couple of hours or more whereas here people begin to get restless if it exceeds the hour. I think it must mean that the African uses up far less nervous energy and takes things as they come. But it also means that he is far more fatalistic in his attitude to life. I know that I generalise and that Western pressures are making inroads on Eastern mentality. That is a great pity for the East can teach us some important lessons.

The extended family is alien to our individualistic approach. Long before we contemplated going to Africa we met in our parish in Kilburn a Nigerian couple who were studying in this country. He later became a well known lawyer and politician in Nigeria. They introduced me to kolanut. You break kolanut in Nigeria as an act of friendship and acceptance. In my innocence I bit into the piece that was offered to me and nearly passed out. It was so bitter. At least I had been warned when we eventually went to Nigeria. I was surprised when I heard that this couple had left their children behind with the grandparents. I could not understand how any parent could part with their children for a year. But in Africa children do not just belong to the parents, but to the wider family and they grow up happily in this family circle. In turn, our Nigerian friends could not understand that we put our elderly relations into Old People's Homes. Such homes do not exist there. The elderly would stay with the extended family and would be looked after by them. When we left Nigeria our students could not understand that we had to go home for the education of our children. But when I mentioned that our parents were getting on and that we needed to be nearer to them they sympathised with this straightaway.

Religion is still part and parcel of the African soul and of society. In educated circles you may now find some who are agnostics. But basically every African has an innate sense of God or at least of the supernatural. The Yoruba religion is dominated by various Gods. To talk about God or religion causes no embarrassment. We feel terribly inhibited in our secular society to talk about spiritual things. Not so the African. Whether Christian, Muslim or animist he lives in a universe in which spiritual forces are active and part of daily life. Many of the buses and lorries which criss-cross the country have religious slogans on them 'The lord is my shepherd' . . ., 'God is our refuge . . .', 'Trust in the Lord . . .'. In the Church there is a greater awareness of God's mercies. Public Thanksgivings play an important part in the worship, hence often the length of the service. When a son has come back from the UK with some academic award or when a member of the family has recovered from an illness the whole family will dance up to the altar and offer thanks, usually with a special collection. Dancing is a natural expression of joy and praise. We have much to learn from their spontaneous and uninhibited faith.

This widespread and genuine faith is reflected in the life of the Church. In most places the Churches are full to overflowing. Confirmations are often in terms of hundreds rather than tens. Since we were there many Churches all over the country have been rebuilt on a larger scale to accommodate the steadily increasing numbers. The number of dioceses has doubled, if not trebled since the fifties. Whereas here Church attendance has been steadily falling there it is increasing by leaps and bounds. I wonder whether in the next century the centre of Christianity will be in Africa rather than the West. One felt very privileged to belong to such a vibrant Church.

Obviously life was not all a bed of roses. There were many daily frustrations.Many things did not work properly. Suddenly there was only a trickle in the tap and you knew that the water went off. Or the electricity broke down. Or the steward who was helping in the house was unreliable. There was the constant heat and humidity which were trying and enervating. There was the widespread problem of corruption. You had to give a 'dash' before anyone was prepared to do anything for you. And this was much worse for the local people who often would not be seen at the hospital or issued with medicines until they had bribed the porter or attendant. Victor, one of our bright students, was going to England for further training and needed a passport. He went down to Lagos and queued up at the Passport Office, but they wanted a bribe. He refused and stood his ground for five days before they finally gave in. He was a stubborn Christian and would not compromise his principles. Most people would give in on the first day for the sake of convenience. We Europeans see corruption as a terrible thing. In the East it is an acceptable way of life. Anger and the 'dark eye' is considered a far greater sin.

There were days when we found life quite unbearable, mainly because of the climate. But in retrospect we gained so much in the seven years that it far outweighed the difficulties and frustrations we encountered. Fortunately, we kept in good health most of the time and the children thrived. And the work of training men for the Christian ministry was immensely worthwhile. We must have made many blunders, especially in not understanding another culture. But hopefully we also contributed something to the upbuilding of the Church. We arrived back in England at the beginning of December. Graeme Spiers, my bestman, now a Vicar in Liverpool, met us and took us to see Clifford Martin, his Bishop, who prayed with us and for our future. It was a good beginning to our homecoming.

# 12

# Liskeard Lodge, Chislehurst (1964–1969)

WE came back to a very different world from the one we had left only seven years earlier. Entering the world of the Sixties seemed as though what had gone before belonged to the Middle Ages. 1963 when we came home was almost a watershed both for society at large as also for the Church. It was the beginning of the Permissive Society. But also several significant developments were taking place in the Church. The Second Vatican Council under Pope John XXIII began in October 62 and went on for three years. It suddenly brought the Roman Church into the 20th Century with some breathtaking changes. In March 63 an article by the Bishop of Woolwich, John Robinson, with the title 'Our image of God must go' appeared in the *Observer* and caused a great stir. It was followed by his book which led to the lively *Honest to God* debate. Also in 1963 the Charismatic Movement began in this country led by a Curate from All Souls, Langham Place.

Following the creation of the Church of South India we heard of a new liturgy, that of the CSI. Perhaps under its influence John Robinson (before he became Bishop) introduced a special liturgy at Clare College, Cambridge. They were the forerunners of the liturgical experiments and reforms within the Church in the Sixties. Almost overnight, the Vatican Council changed the liturgy of the Roman Church from the Latin Mass to the vernacular.

There were then a number of radical and unsettling changes within the Church when we came home – a new morality (if one could call it that), a new theology, a new liturgy. I am still not sure what brought it all about and why just in the 1960s. Right up to the late Fifties there had been a veneer of respectability and traditionalism. The Church seemed to be stable. Numbers of Confirmations and Ordinations were still high and the forecast indicated that this would continue. But underneath that facade there was a hollowness which sooner or later had to be faced. If the Church was to be honest to itself questions had to be asked. The new culture of permissiveness asked many uncomfortable questions. And the Church was not shielded from this trend. From now on many radical questions were being asked and experiments were being made to make the Church relevant to the society of the second half of the century. 'Relevance' became the in-word.

We were very fortunate that we did not have to start looking for a job. Before we left Nigeria Max Warren had asked us whether we were prepared to join the Staff of the CMS Training College, Liskeard Lodge, at Chislehurst. Since we had been in training there in 1955–56 new buildings had been added to accommodate the large number of candidates. We moved straight into a Staff flat in one of the new buildings. Dennis Runcorn was the Principal, Jim Hewitt the Vice-Principal, and I became the Chaplain. The wives were also quite involved in the training. As before, we had quite a close link with Foxbury down the road where the women were trained. There was a constant traffic up and down Kemnal Road for joint lectures, social events and sometimes even romances between the single men and women. Living in community had its pros and cons. It gave Staff and students the rare opportunity to practice the degree of fellowship that is sadly denied to most Christians. We normally meet in Church on a Sunday for about an hour as the 'Body of Christ' and then disperse for the rest of the week. The Body of Christ largely ceases to exist from Monday to Saturday. It is only within a resident Christian community that you can experience 'koinonia' properly. There is a richness and intensity about that fellowship when you live and work and worship and play together week in, week out. But inevitably it also has its strains and stresses. You have to live alongside people that you may find difficult to get on with. Even among Christians there are people whom you would not choose to live and work with day by day. Living at close quarters you soon discover each other's strong and weak points and that can be very trying at times. In our case it was not just a question of one year's training. We lived in community for six years. That taught us some hard, but also helpful lessons.

There were not only temperamental differences between us, but – what proved more painful – differences as Christians. Among the students we had some who were very conservative evangelicals and others who had a more liberal outlook. They sometimes found it difficult to see eye to eye with each other. The most painful experience was when the charismatic movement first 'hit' the College. A fellow curate of Michael Harper at All Souls, Langham Place came into training. He and his wife were a lovely Christian couple. They had recently experienced this new manifestation of the Holy Spirit in their lives and were speaking in tongues. Through their influence some of the other students had this pentecostal experience, too. Before long it led to a deep and painful split within the College. There were those who believed that they had come into a fuller blessing of the Spirit and were anxious to impart it to the rest. In consequence, those who did not respond to this pressure and did not feel that they needed this further blessing were almost regarded as second class citizens. There were many painful discussions, it brought discord into the community. This was in the early days of the charismatic movement when its proponents were not always very tolerant and their approach was a little crude. Within a Christian community it proved very divisive. This unhappy episode was probably one of the most distressing experiences in the course of my ministry.

By the time we came home Max Warren had left CMS and had been succeeded by John Taylor. As previously when we were in training ourselves he and other Secretaries of the Society came down to Chislehurst from time to time. I remember vividly that when one of us had collected John from the Station he would ask to be left alone in the Library for a few minutes before the lecture. He then came out of the Library at the last minute with a few headings jotted down on the back of an envelope and then proceeded to give a most stimulating lecture. We had various other speakers as well. Archbishop Anthony Bloom came more than once. At one of his visits our David was on his way home from school. A car pulled up alongside him and a man in black with a long beard and a deep voice leaned out of the car window to ask the way to Liskeard Lodge. David took fright at the sight of this strange man and ran off! Dr Frank Luke came each year to run a course on Clinical Theology. We also had Terry Waite long before he became well known. He was then a Church Army Captain and had done some work in group dynamics. He shared his insights with us.

A lasting learning experience both for Jean and me was our involvement with Bruce Reed and Christian Teamwork. As our training was so much concerned with human relationships we, the Staff, tried constantly to enlarge our understanding of it. Some of us attended Group Dynamic Courses run by Christian Teamwork. The learning and self-discovery that took place in these courses was considerable. The sessions were intense, concentrated and at times extremely painful. But we learnt a great deal about the way we tick in group behaviour. It was an important stage in our lives and I have certainly never been quite the same since.

We decided to run a course for both Colleges because of what we had learnt and because of the light it threw on relationships. We made that decision after very careful consideration. We realised that there was a risk in putting our students through this kind of learning process. It was a very intense week led by Bruce Reed and his team. Some of the students found it very helpful, others hated it. There was a girl from Foxbury who simply could not cope with it and was in some distress. I remember going to a weekend CMS Conference in the middle of the course at Eastbourne. Sir Kenneth Grubb, the President of CMS, was there. There had been a request to him that the course should be stopped immediately. But we argued that one could not interrupt it in the middle with a great deal of unfinished business. We were allowed to complete the course, but it was touch and go. I think that this girl would not have coped overseas. This learning experience, however bitter it was, made her realise that she was not ready for the demands that the missionfield would make on her.

In 1964 I went as one of the CMS delegates to the Nottingham Faith and Order Conference. We were 500 delegates from all the British Churches. It was one of the biggest and most important ecumenical gatherings in the British Isles in this century. All the great ecumenical leaders were present. It renewed my longing for the unity of the Church, all the more

when on the last day we passed a solemn resolution for a
Covenant of Unity of all the Churches in this land by 1980.
This was the wording of the resolution:

> United in our urgent desire for One Church Renewed for
> Mission, this Conference invites the member churches of the
> British Council of Churches, in appropriate groupings such as
> nations, to covenant together to work and pray for the inaugura-
> tion of union by a date agreed amongst them.
>
> We dare to hope that this date should not be later than Easter
> Day 1980. We believe we should offer obedience to God in a
> commitment as decisive as this.

I reprint it here in full because we really believed at Nottingham
that we had been given a vision that this was within our reach
and that it was possible to achieve unity in our time. The
resolution was not passed lightly. 1980 then seemed quite a
long way off and we assumed that in the ecumenical climate of
that time such a goal could be reached within sixteen years.
Alas, thirteen years after that target date we are no nearer to
such unity, in fact probably further away than we were at
Nottingham. There are many experiments in co-operation,
certainly at the local level and with the active participation of
the Roman Church, but the vision of organic union that we
cherished at Nottingham seems to have evaporated for the
time being. It was certainly a very inspiring experience to be
present at that historic conference even when in the end
nothing came of that final resolution.

Halfway through our time at Liskeard Lodge Dennis Runcorn left and I succeeded him as Principal. Foxbury, the
Women's College, closed down or rather became the Fellowship House of CMS and all training was now based on
Liskeard Lodge. It meant quite an adjustment in the domestic
arrangements of the College. I also had to find a completely
new Staff. I was very fortunate in bringing together a good
team – another family, and two women who had worked in
East Africa. As our students ranged from conservative evangelical to a broader and more liberal churchmanship it was
important to have a balance of theological positions among
the Staff. Jean Ely had been a Ruanda missionary and represented the more evangelical side. Joanna Chase had been a
missionary in Kenya and the Hintons had worked in Pakistan.

We were a good team and worked harmoniously together. Sadly some years later, after they had left Liskeard Lodge, Jean Ely died of cancer and Joanna Chase who had returned to Kenya died in a road accident there. It was a new experience for CMS and for us to have all our students in training on the same site. It worked well. We felt that it made much more sense to train men, women and families under the same roof. It created a more complimentary and richer community.

But even the days of joint training at Liskeard Lodge were soon numbered. CMS was one of the few missionary societies who did not share in the Mission training that was provided at Selly Oak, Birmingham. It was very convenient to have the College at Chislehurst which was within easy reach from headquarters in Waterloo Road. There was a natural reluctance to move the college to the Midlands where this close link would not be possible. The training that CMS provided was, as I indicated above, quite distinct in its ethos. There was a fear that this might be lost at Selly Oak. There was a long debate as to the pros and cons, but in the end John Taylor, the General Secretary, decided that the gain of being at the Centre of Mission at Selly Oak far outweighed the loss of proximity to London and of the integrated community life at Chislehurst. Plans were laid for the building of a new College on a site that was still available at Selly Oak. We were closely involved in these plans and paid several visits to Birmingham as the new buildings began to take shape.

The question was whether we would move with the College to Birmingham. Eventually John Taylor invited Simon Barrington-Ward to be Principal of Crowther Hall (the name of the new College there, after Samuel Crowther, the first African Bishop). This made our decision easier. By now we had been with CMS for fourteen years, the last six on the Staff and as Principal at their Training College. It was probably the right moment for us to make a move although we had been extremely happy to belong to the CMS fellowship. Max Warren and John Taylor had been inspiring in their leadership. Their vision and thinking and writing had been a great stimulus for us personally and to the training in general. It was quite a wrench to leave that great family.

So what next? John Robinson was Bishop of Woolwich in

the Diocese of Southwark. Max Warren had been a near neighbour of his at Blackheath. He must have mentioned my named to John Robinson. We were at Lee Abbey at Easter and I had a message to ring Max. We had gone to Barnstaple on that day and I rang him at a pre-arranged time from the Post Office there. He told me that the Bishop of Southwark would shortly be in touch with me to offer me the Parish of St Margaret, Putney. So began twenty-one years of parochial ministry in that part of London, first in Putney and then in Barnes. On 22nd July 1969 we said goodbye to Chislehurst and moved to our new home in Putney. It was the first proper house that we had had in all the seventeen years of our married life.

# 13

# St Margaret's, Putney
# (1969–1981)

In January we had attended the funeral of Wilfred Brown at St Margaret's, Putney. Wilfred had been our tutor at Liskeard Lodge some thirteen years earlier. He and Joan, his wife, were held in great affection by many people. When he left Chislehurst he went to St Matthew's, Newington, a very tough area near the Elephant and Castle. When we were back at Liskeard Lodge on the Staff some of our students used to go to St Matthew's for some pastoral work. In 1966 the Browns moved to St Margaret's, Putney. Sadly, three years later at Christmas Wilfred had a sudden heart attack and died. A newly ordained deacon had only just joined him as Curate and then nobly held the fort during the interregnum. Little did we guess when we attended Wilfred's funeral that six months later I would succeed him.

We were very fortunate that we were called to live and work in that part of London. It is a very pleasant area with Wimbledon Common and Richmond Park and Kew Gardens all within easy reach. And we both knew it fairly well. When I lived at Fulham and worked in an office at Wimbledon I used to cycle through Putney. Jean's home was (and still is) at Wandsworth Common and she also knew that part of the world well. St Margaret's is a large Parish which after the first war was carved out of Putney Parish when large new estates sprang up between Putney and Roehampton. The Parish consisted of three distinct areas – the older Dover House Estate with cottage type of Council Housing which in the early twenties was a showcase; the more recent Ashburton Estate mainly with blocks of flats; and the more expensive area towards the centre of Putney where many professional people lived. The Church was actually right in the middle of it all, tucked away on an unmade up lane. Most people did not even know that there was a Church, it was so out of the way and difficult to get to. It had a rather quaint history. It began as a private chapel belonging to one of the big houses in Putney before the beginning of the century and was then mainly attended by the servants of some of the big houses around there. For a time it became a Presbyterian Church and then a daughter Church of Putney Parish when it was refurbished in a more Anglican style. On the outside it still looks like a country chapel.

There I was inducted by Mervyn Stockwood, the Bishop of Southwark, on St James' Day 1969. It was, of course, quite a shock to the system to become an Incumbent after having been out of parish work for 14 years. It was a challenge to launch into this new venture. I remember the very able Rector of St Nicholas, Chislehurst where I used to assist quite regularly on Sundays saying to me once that I would never make a good parish priest. Here was my opportunity to prove him wrong!

I began by visiting all the members of the Church Council, leaders of the organisations and other key members of the congregation. I soon got to know quite a large number of Church members. Again as in my curacy at Kilburn I discovered how much people appreciate it when you take the time and trouble to visit them. There was quite a good congregation when I arrived, but gradually over the years we saw many new faces. That was encouraging at a time when Churchgoing was on the decline. Most of them came from the more professional area. We had many friendly contacts with people from the Dover House Estate who in the past used to go to Church and still considered St Margaret's as 'their' Church. But nothing would induce them to come back again. The newer of the two Estates, the Ashburton, was even more difficult. We had a tiny Sunday School there to have a presence on the Estate. At one of my first Christmasses in the parish we decided to have a Carol Service on the Estate. We circulated every flat and house on the Estate, we booked the Community Hall. The few Churchmembers who lived there were quite sure that there would be a good turnout. In the end apart from our regular members we had a few mums and their children. We were so sure that a Carol Service would appeal, but even that did not draw them away from the pub or the television.

Liturgically, we were just at the beginning of a diet of little booklets which eventually led up to *The Alternative Service Book* (ASB) of 1980. In 1969 I think we were on Series 1 soon moving on to Series 2. The Roman Church after the Second Vatican Council had made the change all in one. Almost overnight they had changed to the vernacular which for them was even more radical after their services in Latin. The Church of England progressed much more slowly and democratically. As much as I appreciate the Book of Common Prayer and its beautiful language I welcomed the innovation. I felt that the quaint old language fixed the Church of England in the past. I was anxious to present an image of the Church which was contemporary and which spoke in the language of our time. But I also welcomed it because in the Prayer Book the Eucharist dwells almost exclusively on the Cross and the sacrifice of Christ. This is, of course, quite a valid interpretation of the meaning of the Holy Communion. But there is hardly a reference to the glorious and complimentary truths of the Gospel, i.e. Christ's resurrection and ascension nor to the third person of the Trinity, the Holy Spirit. The revised services gave us a much more comprehensive range of God's saving work. So from the beginning I was fully in sympathy with the rather exciting liturgical reform. I welcomed it as a sign of new life within the Church, not only the Anglican Church, but right across the denominations. I was pleased when the PCC agreed to adopt Series 3, the forerunner of Rite A. Some of our people were quite intrigued at that time when they attended an ecumenical service at the local Roman Church and found that their Mass in structure if not in wording was almost the same as ours.

From the beginning I was very keen to foster good ecumenical relationships with the neighbouring churches. We had an active Putney Council of Churches which arranged a number of ecumenical events. I mentioned earlier that when I was in Kilburn one hardly greeted the Roman priest if one met him in the street and we certainly had no contacts with their local church. Now twenty years later and after Vatican II this had changed and the Roman Church was a member of our Council of Churches. Towards the end of my time at Putney we had a new younger and very energetic priest at St Simon's, the Roman Church, with whom I got on extremely well. One of my real regrets on leaving Putney was that our close understanding and co-operation came to an end.

We had particularly close relations with the United Reformed Church which was within the parish. Again soon after my arrival they had a new young and delightful minister. When I was invited to preach there I was without question asked to assist in the administration of the Holy Communion. In the diocese of Southwark one was encouraged to follow one's own conscience.

One Sunday I invited this United Reformed minister to preach at our Eucharist and then to assist with the communion. On Saturday afternoon a fairly new member of the congregation with a legal background presented himself at the Vicarage and threatened that if I went ahead with Raymond's participation in the Holy Communion he would make a public protest during the service and would try to stop it. I was in a dilemma. I was anxious to go ahead with this demonstration of Christian unity. On the other hand I certainly did not want to have a public disturbance in the middle of a solemn Eucharist. I rang the Bishop of Kingston to seek his advice. He was very sympathetic, but left the decision to me. In the end I decided to call it off and rang Raymond and explained my dilemma to him. He was very gracious and understanding. He came and preached, but did not take part in the administration. From now on I was pursued by this same man whenever I did not keep to the straight and narrow path. It was very trying. He became a thorn in my flesh during the remainder of my time at Putney. In the end the Bishop of Southwark summoned us both to Bishop's House and having heard us told my opponent in no uncertain terms that he had no time for him and that he was to leave me in peace.

This was rather typical of Mervyn Stockwood. He was a somewhat flamboyant man and larger than life. He could be very stern if you crossed him, but generally speaking he was very good with his clergy and, as in this case, would stand up for them and support them. I soon realised how lucky I was to be in his diocese. It was an exciting place and there was a lot going on. It may have been radical and at times unorthodox ('Southbank theology' has its origin here). For some it was too liberal. But life in Southwark was never dull. It was stimulating and at times entertaining. And that was largely due to the kind of leadership that Mervyn Stockwood gave. He made some good appointments – David Sheppard at Woolwich (after John Robinson), Hugh Montefiore at Kingston.

I remember that when the appointment of Montefiore was first announced in the diocese my Rural Dean (an Evangelical) wrote an article in his Church Magazine denouncing the appointment. This was because of a passing reference to Jesus as a homosexual that he had made in a lecture. There were others who were uneasy about the appointment for the same reason. At the next Diocesan Synod Dr Stockwood asked Hugh Montefiore to appear to introduce himself and to explain the context in which he had made that remark which the press had picked up. He came over so well and made such a masterly defence that very quickly people dropped their reservations. Hugh became a very popular Bishop in the diocese. Our Rural Dean soon changed his mind!

When I became Rural Dean of Wandsworth we were invited from time to time to some of Mervyn's parties at Bishop's House. He loved parties (hence my reference above to life in Southwark being entertaining) and there was usually plenty of food and drink, perhaps too much. But his parties were fun and provided good opportunities to meet some of the other clergy and their wives in an informal and relaxed atmosphere. At one of the Christmas Parties (Hugh Montefiore had gone to Birmingham) the Bishop like a magician produced Keith Sutton as the next Bishop of Kingston. We had known Keith and Jean and their children since Liskeard days when they were in training with us before going out to the theological College at Mukono in Uganda. Then they returned to Cambridge where Keith became Principal of Ridley Hall. Now we suddenly found that our former student was our new Bishop. Keith had been recommended to Mervyn who promptly went up to Cambridge to meet Keith and then offered him the post. I don't know what Keith made of this first introduction to Southwark Diocese in the middle of a rather noisy Christmas Party!

The Bishop was also very keen for Rural Deans to entertain their clergy to create a sense of fellowship and support when clergy could easily be lonely and isolated in their parishes.

When I was Rural Dean we had an annual party for the clergy and their wives in the Deanery which I think was appreciated by everybody who came. I enjoyed the seven years while I was Rural Dean. It increased the workload, but it brought me into closer touch with the diocese and with the other parishes in the Deanery. We used to have the occasional Rural Deans' meetings at which some of the problems and projects in the diocese were threshed out. But the greatest value I found was the contact with the congregations and their representatives in the Churches in Wandsworth. I was involved when there were interregnums. I used to visit the churches for the annual Visitation, I was invited to preach in the other churches from time to time. Some of the visits were mainly concerned with legalities and with bricks and mortar, but in the course of these visits one also heard of some of the needs and problems that faced some of the congregations and one could offer encouragement and advice.

I got involved in the Diocese in other ways, too. Southwark used to run a very good Pastoral Care and Counselling network. There were a number of groups throughout the diocese which consisted of clergy, layfolk, Social Workers to look critically and honestly at some of the personal and interpersonal relationships that we all come up against from time to time. Usually a member of the group would bring a case and then we would look at it together and discuss it. It was helpful because a group could often throw light on the problem and analyse it. For a time two of us used to run the local group. In addition the leaders of all the groups in the diocese would regularly meet under the leadership of a psychiatrist at St George's Hospital and raise some of the issues that we had examined in our local groups. As with Christian Teamwork I gained some useful insights into human behaviour from these groups.

Another project in the Deanery which occupied me was Lay Training. For several years I was involved in the planning and running of Deanery Lay Training Courses. They were both doctrinal and practical. At the end of a year's Course there was a Service at which the Bishop would formally recognise members who had passed the requirements as Pastoral Assistants. It was quite time-consuming drawing up these Courses and finding the right people to run the various sessions. We usually began the evenings with a Eucharist and then moved on to the particular topic for the week. I was always impressed with the commitment of the participants. Most of them were busy people in their own professions and also in their parishes. But the attendance record was very high and showed how much such training and learning was appreciated. So was the experience of Christians from different Churches and Churchmanships working together on a joint project. There was always the problem of ending. In the course of their training they had become a very committed group and found it hard to part. Here I caught a glimpse of the Christian Church at its best and most constructive performance.

Back in the parish Jean and I launched a Youth Group. They used to meet in the our Vicarage on a Sunday evening and within a short period of time we had a full house. At one of our first meetings we had our Bishop, Hugh Montefiore, as speaker. Our sitting room was absolutely packed. One Christmas the Youth Group produced a concert which was brilliant and was a great success. The talent among these youngsters was quite remarkable. They also organised their own regular Bible Study. It was exciting to see young people these days so committed to the Christian Faith. The Group went on for some three years. Then suddenly overnight they all went off to College and University. It never took off again as it had done that first time.

One nightmare while we were in Putney will always stay in my mind. We used to have a rota for Confirmations for the three Anglican Churches in Putney and Roehampton. One year it was our turn and it was held in February. It was a very cold spell. I went over to the Church on the Saturday evening to check that everything was in order for the following morning when the Bishop of Kingston would come to take the Confirmation. To my surprise the heating was not on and the Church felt very cold. Our dear old Verger who looked after the heating had been out during the day and I assumed that he had perhaps forgotten to set it. I checked with him as soon as he got home and he was equally surprised that it was not working. It was a very old boiler. We tried everything to light it, but nothing happened. The boiler had broken down just when we needed it most. What were we to do? I rang an emergency number. They turned up quite late on Saturday evening and got to work in the bowels of the earth where the boiler was. They took it to pieces. It took several hours. I hovered round them getting more and more anxious. We supplied them with cups of tea to encourage them. But at about 3 am we gave up. We were going to catch a few hours' sleep and try again in the morning. But next morning it became quite clear that we were not going to have any heat in the Church for the Service. I felt dreadful, especially as we were the hosts on this occasion and there would be many visitors. It was too late to cancel the Confirmation or transfer it to another church. We rang round to members of the congregation asking them to bring any portable heaters. It took the chill off, but I can't say that we were very comfortable. Hugh, our Bishop, took it in good part. As we came to the end of the service we could hear some ticking in the radiators. The engineers had at long last coaxed the boiler into life. But, I am afraid it was too late for the Confirmation and the final bill was several hundred pounds!

As the years went by I felt less and less happy about the preparation for Baptisms and Marriages. These were two vital events in the lives of parents and couples and yet because of so many other commitments one gave far too little time to them. In those days videos were not yet in vogue, but one of our leading laymen was an expert in producing beautiful slide shows of their holidays. With his help we produced a very good home-grown filmstrip on Baptism with a running commentary. We also trained a number of Baptism visitors. We would then invite the parents of children shortly to be baptised to come to an evening of Baptism preparation. There we would show the filmstrip and then invite discussion. These evenings were useful. They demonstrated that we took the christening of their children seriously and that we were concerned that the parents should take it seriously, too, which was by no means always the case.

Jean and I also started up Marriage Preparation Groups. We invited several couples who were shortly getting married to come for two or sometimes three evenings. We had an internal agenda of questions that we wanted to raise with them which

*On a College Mission upcountry in Nigeria with staff and students*

*The rebuilt St. Mary's, Barnes*

*Henry Ball (left) on a visit to England 1991*

led on to a general discussion. We found that most of them were extremely nervous when they first came. Little did they know that we were just as apprehensive because we realised that these sessions had to be handled very delicately. But as the first evening went on everybody became more relaxed and by the time they left us on the second or third evening we all knew each other fairly well and they appreciated the work we had done together. It is impossible to know what effect this preparation will have had, but at least we enabled these couples to look at their future relationships through the experience of two people who had tested both the ups and downs of married life. We found it one of the most demanding things we had done together, but for that reason probably all the more worthwhile.

Quite early on in Putney I introduced an annual all day PCC Conference in addition to the monthly PCC meetings. This gave the PCC the opportunity to discuss at greater length and leisure some of the bigger issues affecting our parish or the Church at large. For this conference we usually met somewhere outside the parish. A different venue helped to give our deliberations a more relaxed tone. There was always a Eucharist at the end when we passed the bread and wine to each other. So often PCCs are just business meetings. Although the business is necessary, it is also important to convey that the members of the PCC are the spiritual guardians of the local Church and these all day meetings helped to foster that.

We also organised an annual Church House Party, first as Ashburnham Place and then later at Pilgrim Hall, both in Sussex. There were usually several teaching and discussion groups, but in between there was plenty of time to enjoy each other's company and to have fun and games. On the Saturday evening we always had an impromptu concert – music, sketches, readings. I usually invited somebody to lead the House Party. Michael Whinney who was then one of the Archdeacons in Southwark and later became Bishop led our first one. Keith de Berry, former Rector of St Aldate's Oxford and a great evangelist led another one. Their input provided the framework for these weekends, but I think the greatest value was the experience of Christian fellowship. I think it did more than anything else to draw people together and give them a taste of what Christian community can be like. Normally we engage in worship on a Sunday which is, of course, central to the Christian Faith. But we miss out on 'koinonia', 'having all things in common'. When you live and work and worship and play together for a whole weekend you begin to understand in mind and heart what it means to be the Body of Christ. Those who came to these residential weekends often talked about them for weeks afterwards.

One of the greatest privileges and responsibilities of a Parish Priest is to share his experience and skills with those who were only just beginning their ministry. When I arrived in Putney Norman Jeffery, a local 'boy', had held the fort during the interregnum as a deacon and had just been priested. After him there were three other Curates, all very different, but each making his particular contribution and at the same time equipping themselves for their future ministry. We also had a Church Army Captain on the Staff. I still feel that appointing him was probably one of the best things I did in Putney. Tony Maidment and Sylvia, his wife, ran a tough Church Army hostel for delinquent boys in the parish. I dropped in from time to time and got to know them. I felt that he would be just the right person for the pastoral work on our two housing estates. I invited him to join us at St Margaret's. Church Army gave their blessing to this move. Tony with his love for the Lord and his irrepressible humour and just the right touch with people proved a first-class parish worker and was well liked everywhere. He stayed for quite a few years at St Margarets and later specialised in work among children. Today he is a freelance evangelist, still under the auspices of the Church Army, in the Midlands and is much in demand running Children's Missions.

I was also very fortunate in having throughout my time outstanding Churchwardens. It is very important for a fruitful ministry to have the support of good lay leaders. I turned to them to air some of my ideas and also problems with them and seek their advice. Together we could formulate policies before they were presented to the Church Council for their consideration. Several of my Wardens during those years are still our personal friends today.

In 1979 I had a Sabbatical in the States. Until the Seventies I had never heard of sabbaticals in the Church. Now many clergy have the opportunity to go on these extended study leaves at least once in the course of their ministry. And a good thing it is, too. There are plenty of opportunities to go on short courses and conferences to stimulate the mind. Many clergy go on annual retreats. There are many peaceful Retreat Houses all over the country. But all these facilities are of limited benefit and last only for a week or less. Once you are back in the parish with the best will in the world there is precious little time for sustained reading and study. In the course of a ministry of some thirty or forty years there is a real need to have some extended time for thought and study to refresh the mind and to update one's reading. The Church has at long last caught up with the need for sabbaticals. They are a good spiritual investment.

The right use of the Sabbatical is largely left to each individual. I had heard of the Procter Program offered by the Episcopal Divinity School in Cambridge, Massachusetts. I applied and in due course was offered a place. The Bishop found me £200 which more or less covered the airfare. The Procter Program financed the rest of the three months' period of my stay at EDS. So apart from some pocket money I was not out of pocket. I had a good Curate at the time and could safely leave him in charge of the parish while I was away. Towards the end of August I set off. Jean and David joined me for the first three weeks. It was our first visit to USA. We visited friends in New Hampshire and Boston and then paid a fleeting visit to New York and Washington. From there Jean and David flew home and I made my way back to Cambridge for the beginning of the semester.

The Episcopal Divinity School is 'on Brattle Street' near Harvard Square. In a new block are the Lecture Rooms and in the basement a very impressive Library. It has an equally impressive academic Staff of Professors of high calibre. There must have been well over 100 students, some training with the ordained ministry in mind, others to obtain a religious qualification and others, mainly women, just to do some theological education. A number lived in, some had married quarters outside and again others were day students. It felt more like a mini University.

The added advantage of EDS is that it is within walking distance of Harvard University and that it has a close link with the theological department there. I realised very quickly that I was in for a semester of very stimulating study. We were four Procter students that year – a parish priest, a College Chaplain, a nun and myself coming from UK. The Program says in its introduction that 'it provides the opportunity for clergy to strengthen their ministry in a semester of study and renewal'. I found both in full measure during those three months. I had a large number of courses to choose from. It was agonising to limit it to four subjects. For two of them I went over to Harvard, one of them was on other religions and sects and was led by Harvey Cox who in the sixties and seventies became well known through his *Secular City* and other books. Another course on Philosophy I attended at the Weston School of Theology almost next door to EDS which was a remarkably open-minded Roman Catholic Seminary. I indulged in a great deal of reading. I tried to take a full part in the life of the community. I appreciated the worship in the Chapel. I found it quite exciting to be a student again.

My criticism of EDS in no way diminishes my enormous appreciation of my time there. On the whole I found the theological approach too liberal. I was quite horrified with the lectures at Harvard given by a very able German Professor. He demythologised the New Testament to such an extent that there was very little of divine truth left at the end. Among the students at EDS were quite a number of militant 'gays' and also ardent feminists. While both these groups have a contribution to make in the life of the Church I found their stance much too blatant. On the other hand I was delighted to receive ministry from female priests for the first time and certainly found nothing extraordinary in that.

I explored the beautiful city of Boston with its museums and interesting history. I was given a number of contacts before I left England. I also made new friendships and enjoyed the proverbial American hospitality. At weekends I visited some of the contacts I had been given and shared in the worship of quite a number of Churches. I was particularly impressed with the Christian Education Programme of most Churches. Sunday School is by no means limited to children. When the Sunday morning service is over the congregation adjourn for coffee and then disperse to a number of different classes on the Christian Faith. And then they return to their homes for a light lunch. We are so bound by our Sunday dinner that there is no time for further education, to our detriment!

At half term I even managed to fly right across the States to Los Angeles to visit my friend Henry and his wife Vi in their home in Burbank. This gave me a chance to catch a brief glimpse of the West Coast as well. Altogether this Sabbatical proved a very enriching time. I flew back just before Christmas and plunged straight into all the Christmas services.

Towards the end of our time in Putney we had a Mission. It was ecumenical in character. The United Reformed Church took part and the other local Churches supported it. I suggested the retired Bishop of Coventry, Cuthbert Bardsley, as our Missioner. We approached him. The timing had to be delayed because he was not available when we had in mind to run the Mission, but he said 'yes'. That was a real scoop. He was one of the great evangelists in the Church of England. Donald Coggan has paid full tribute to him in his biography of Cuthbert Bardsley. I remember going to a Youth Rally at the Central Hall, Westminster soon after the War. Bardsley was then the Provost of Southwark Cathedral. He was the main speaker at this Rally and nearly raised the roof. I came out of the Hall as he left and I thanked him for his inspiring address. Now over thirty years later he was our Missioner. We held the main mission services in the Hall of Digby Stuart College, the Roman Catholic Teacher Training College in Roehampton. In his typical, slightly theatrical manner Cuthbert Bardsley greeted us at the beginning of each evening with 'The Lord be with you' – three times, each with a different emphasis. Then he proclaimed the Good News of Jesus Christ. And that proclamation was still very powerful.

Prior to the Mission there had been a great deal of planning and publicity and visiting. We had great expectations. It is always difficult to quantify spiritual results. But in terms of number and conversions they were disappointing. The Mission made a great impact on the congregation and a number of our people were renewed in their faith and encouraged in Christian discipleship. But it touched very few outsiders. That seems to be a general experience of most evangelistic efforts in our time. They seem to result in Christian renewal, but not in a breakthrough to the vast majority outside the Church. But for all that it was still worth holding the Mission. And we were very fortunate that Cuthbert Bardsley led it. It was probably one of the last that he conducted.

In our congregation was a man who had recently retired from the BBC World Service and was a brilliant linguist. Almost every other year he tried to learn a new language. In 1975 he was learning Polish and was planning a trip to Poland to try out his newly acquired knowledge. One day he said to me 'You should visit your old hometown Dresden again'. I had not been there since I left it in 1944. A year later it was destroyed. Now it was in the German Democratic Republic and cut off from the rest of the world by the wall that divided East from West. David was planning to go to Poland via Dresden and invited me to go with him. He would leave me in Dresden and he would move on to Poland.

I had to apply in good time for a Visa to East Germany and was required to stay in a state owned hotel. In this way the Communist authorities could keep an eye on visitors from the West. We travelled via Berlin which again I had not seen since the war. The visit to Dresden was a rather depressing pilgrimage. A few of the historic buildings had been restored, but most of them were still in ruins. The centre had been rebuilt, but with plain and unattractive edifices. The character of the Old Market and the main shopping street had completely gone. The shops were largely empty or were stocked with just basic necessitites. The newspaper kiosks were empty except for the Communist papers. For several days I walked round the city trying to find the old familiar landmarks. Our old home had disappeared, in its place stood now a school. St Luke's church where I was confirmed was still there except for the two spires. I called at Church House next to the Church where the pastor used to live and to my delight was greeted by Peter Rietzsch, the present minister. The house had been repaired and they lived in the same flat which I knew so well from earlier days. Peter and Gudrun Rietzsch invited me to their home and out of this chance encounter grew a friendship which still continues With very few exceptions nobody was allowed out of East Germany into the West. The Rietzsches like so many of their fellow countrymen in the East felt cut off from the world. When I left Dresden I was determined to find ways and means of bringing them over to England at the first possible opportunity.

I was in Dresden during the Russian Orthodox Easter. Before midnight the Rietzsches took me to the Russian Orthodox Church which was in St Luke's parish and which strangely had not been damaged in the raids. There right in the heart of a Socialist (Communist) State we celebrated in Russian the resurrection of Christ. I was told afterwards that several Russian officers in mufti were among the worshippers. It was a moving and memorable service.

On my way back from Dresden I stopped off for the night in East Berlin and found a room in the Hotel Adlon near the Brandenburg Gate. The Hotel had seen better days. Before the war it was famous. Foreign royalty and statesmen used to stay there. Now it was terribly run down and a shadow of its former self. Next morning I took a brief stroll Unter Den Linden and past the former Chancellery where Hitler had ended his life when the Russians entered Berlin. Then I crossed over to the West. The contrast between the two sides was incredible. The East dreary and austere, very little traffic, only Trabant cars. West Berlin pulsating with life, the shops bulging with goods, every other car a Mercedes. I did not think that I would ever go back to Dresden while it was under the Communists, but in fact I did, six months before the Wall came down.

1980 was the 75th anniversary of the creation of Southwark Diocese. A big celebration was planned. The organisers succeeded in hiring the Centre Court at Wimbledon just after the championships that year and held a big Open Air Service there. Mervyn Stockwood, our Bishop, was retiring later in the year and so unofficially this was also going to be his swansong.

These celebrations made me think of Peter Rietzsch. Supposing we could pretend that he would be welcomed as a delegate of the Church in East Germany he might be able to get a Visa to come over to England. I put the idea to the Bishop who went along with it. A formal invitation was issued. The German Church authorities made an application to the appro-

priate East German Ministry and now we had to wait. At the
very last minute the Visa was issued to Peter, but not to his
wife. One day in July 1980 I met him off the boat train at
Liverpool Station. He had a fortnight in this country and spent
most of his time sightseeing. He is still talking about this visit.
It was his first opportunity of experiencing the free world since
he was born. For the anniversary celebrations of the Diocese
he sat with the Bishop and other VIPs and witnessed the
highlight of the afternoon when Bishop Mervyn did a lap of
honour round the Centre Court cheered by the thousands of
representatives from all the parishes in the diocese.

By now I had been at St Margaret's for eleven years. I felt
that I had probably accomplished as much as I could there and
the time had come to look for a move. The Bishop had offered
me one or two other parishes in the diocese. We looked at
them, but did not feel that they would be the right ones for us.
They were very much like St Margaret's and did not seem to
offer any special challenge for what was probably going to be
our last parish before retirement. Once or twice I had heard
through the grapevine that the neighbouring Church at Barnes
was at a rather low ebb. I could not quite understand that as I
knew that Barnes was a thriving community and one would
have expected the Church to be doing well, too.

In June 1978 we heard the sad news that the old Parish
Church of Barnes had been completely destroyed by fire. I got
in touch with the Churchwardens and asked whether there
was anything we could do to help. I think we gave them a set
of Prayer Books. In March 1981 the Rector of St Mary's,
Barnes, died. I had seen him briefly for the first and last time
only three weeks earlier when he had brought two of his
candidates to our Confirmation. He struck me as a very sick
man and looked like a ghost. It might have just crossed my
mind that here was indeed the challenge I was looking for – to
go to Barnes and to rebuild the Church and the life of that
congregation. But, of course, I dismissed this from my mind. It
was not normal practice to move to an adjacent parish. It
would not be wise.

It came, therefore, as a great surprise when one day in May
Keith Sutton, who was then the Bishop of Kingston, rang me
and asked whether I would consider going to Barnes. He

dismissed my objection that it was too close to Putney. It was more important to find the right man to take on this difficult job. All the more difficult as there raged a local controversy about the rebuilding of the Church. However, I felt at once that this was the right place for me and that it could be an exciting venture under God.

I was 57 and I think that when the Churchwardens at Barnes heard of my age they had some reservations. I went over to meet them in June. They must have approved of me. And I on my part felt confirmed in my earlier response. The living was in the gift of the Dean and Chapter of St Paul's Cathedral. I had to appear before them. One member of the Chapter was Douglas Webster, my former tutor at College and now a Canon at St Paul's. I was formally accepted by them.

In September we had our farewell at St Margaret's. Christopher Jones, my Curate, recited 'Juergen's Little List' with apologies to Gilbert and Sullivan. He had only been with us for over a year and had just been priested. He was a very good pastor and preacher and I knew that with strong backup from the laity he would see the parish through the interregnum. So we left Putney after more than twelve years with some regrets, but also with eager anticipation of a new beginning in Barnes, just two miles down the road.

# 14

# St Mary's, Barnes
# (1981–1990)

BARNES is a natural community within the loop of the River. It is off the main traffic arteries, and not quite as much disrupted by traffic as Putney or other parts of London. It is still a village and local people refer to it as such. Because of its position there is a real sense of community and it has a very active Community Association.

When you walk along Church Road and the High Street you are bound to meet people you know. That is sadly no longer the case in some other faceless and anonymous parts of London. Fairly close to the centre of Barnes stands the old Parish Church with a great deal of history. It is said that Archbishop Stephen Langton of Canterbury on his river journey back to Lambeth from signing the Magna Carta at Runnymead in 1215 stopped off and consecrated the first Church. But it probably goes back even earlier. The first incumbent was sent there from St Paul's Cathedral in 1199. The Dean and Chapter endowed the living and have remained its Patrons. A number of illustrious and interesting Rectors have been there who have been chronicled in John Whale's book *One Church, One Lord* (SCM Press 1979). The most famous of the Rectors was probably John Ellerton who wrote the famous hymn 'The day thou gavest, Lord, is ended'. I found it very exciting to enter into that apostolic succession.

The previous Rector had been there for eighteen years, but almost right from the beginning he did not seem to be the right 'persona' for that parish. Over the years parishioners drifted away to other Churches and the congregation shrank. Several times the Bishop tried to persuade the Rector to move, but without success. And then the big blow fell. One June evening in 1978 the old Church went up in flames. Talking to people in Barnes it was interesting that as with Kennedy's assassination most of them could still clearly remember what they were doing that evening when the black smoke rose over Barnes. It was a big shock not only for the congregation, but for the whole community. Even if they did not attend the Church, in a village like Barnes, the Church was very much part of everybody. This fire was the last straw of an unhappy period.

Fortunately the Church has a good Hall just round the corner and the services were transferred there. The Hall became the Church for the next six years. When I arrived there was still a core of some 50–60 faithful and committed people. And this was largely due to the loving and dedicated work of Viera Gray. Viera and I met up again in Barnes after some 25 years. We had been in training together in Chislehurst. Viera who was a nurse went with the Ruanda Mission to East Africa. She subsequently came home to look after her mother in Barnes and helped out in the parish. Then she trained as a deaconess and came back to Barnes to work full time in the parish. It was largely due to her caring and tireless ministry that there was a congregation at all.

I was told that one of the last things that Mervyn Stockwood did before he retired at the end of October 1980 was to carry out a 'Visitation' to the then Rector with the intent of imposing a prohibition of exercising his ministry at Barnes. From what I can gather it was quite a dramatic episode. One evening accompanied by the Bishop of Kingston, the Archdeacon of Wandsworth and his Chaplain the Bishop rang the bell at the Rectory and demanded to see the Rector. A few moments later the daughter returned to say that the Rector was not available. There was nothing that the episcopal delegation could do but to turn back. Instead they posted a notice on the Church Door to the effect that the Rector was barred from the Church premises. This, however, was rescinded by the Archbishop of Canterbury when Dr Stockwood retired. And the Rector continued in office until he died some six months later.

When I left Putney I made it quite clear to the congregation of St Margaret's that as much as I loved them their place was to stay and support their Church and not to come across to Barnes which was only fifteen minutes' walk away. Fortunately Barnes Common acts as a natural divide. I would have been very embarrassed if people had followed me.

On 8th October 1981 I was instituted by the Bishop of

Kingston. This service, of course, had to take place in the Church Hall. Douglas Webster representing St Paul's Cathedral presented me and preached the sermon. The Induction had to take place in the Church. It was hardly wise to conduct that ceremony that same evening in the dark as the Church was still a shell and debris was everywhere. So I had the unusual experience that next morning on a misty, moisty October day in the presence of a small group of my new parishioners I was duly inducted by the Archdeacon in the ruins of St Mary's.

The Rectory was in a poor state. Nothing had been done to it during the eighteen years of my predecessor's residence there. We were told to look for some other suitable property in Barnes. But there was nothing on the market that seemed right and in the end we decided to hang on to the existing Rectory. I am glad we did. We spent nine very happy years in it. Quite a lot of alterations had to be made. Fortunately we could stay on in the Putney Vicarage while the work was carried out and for five months I commuted to Barnes several times a day.

The congregation had got themselves remarkably well organised since the fire. As the Hall was used during the week by Cubs and Scouts and other organisations every Saturday morning a squad moved in to sweep the Hall and set out the chairs for the Services on Sunday. An ordinary dining room table served as altar. Some candle stands had been preserved from the fire, so had the vestments. Sunday evenings after Evensong the whole process had to be reversed. It was a tedious weekly routine, but one soon got used to it.

At a pinch we could seat up to 150 people. As we were then still a relatively small congregation the seating was no problem. But one day we nearly lost our altar! Once a year the Scouts had an enormous Jumble Sale the like of which I had never come across before. The Hall was stacked high with every conceivable item for sale. The table that served as our altar was kept in a corner of the stage. When the Hall was cleared at the end of the Jumble Sale on the Saturday afternoon our altar had disappeared. It had been sold! We managed to trace the new owner who was already in the process of stripping the top. Well, we go it back less part of the veneer. But as the table was covered with the altar cloth that did not matter.

The task before me now was to rebuild the Church both

materially and spiritually. I came to Barnes with some twelve years behind me of running a parish, but the rebuilding of an ancient church from the ashes was a completely new challenge. Of the former church only the walls and the tower were standing. The interior which was open to the elements was a sorry sight. Apart from the immediate clearing up after the fire it had been left with all its debris for over three years and I really began to wonder where to begin. But this was not the immediate problem.

A fierce controversy was raging over the plans for the new Church which seemed to split the local community even more than the congregation. The Church Council and the Rebuilding Committee had asked an architect, Ted Cullinan, to draw up a design and after careful consideration of the scheme they had adopted it. It was imaginative, it blended some of the old features with a completely new structure, it moved the altar area from the traditional east to the north. It represented a radical reordering of the building which related the past to the future. The scheme was violently opposed by a group of people, mainly on the fringe of the congregation, who called themselves the 'Within the Walls' committee. They wanted the Church rebuilt more or less as it had been before the fire and strictly within the existing walls. They had appointed their own architect who had produced his own traditional scheme within the walls.

Before I arrived in Barnes there had been public meetings which had been acrimonious and confrontational. Some members of the congregation were afraid to go out because they were exposed to verbal abuse. It was all very unpleasant. There had even been a Consistory Court in Barnes over which the Bishop presided, but it had not cleared the air. I could tell when I appeared on the scene that the atmosphere was charged and that I was going to have a very tough problem on my hands. I was soon approached by the opposition who hoped that they could win me over to their side. I met the two leaders of the group who opposed the scheme and found them quite fanatical in their determination to stop Ted Cullinan's design from going ahead.

I tried to keep an open mind, but I certainly liked the design. It was creative and forward looking. I was convinced

that here was an opportunity which few other Churches have
– at the end of the century to produce something new rather
than to be dominated by the past. I was impressed with the
Rebuilding Committee, especially the Chairman who was a
fairly high powered businessman and who had vision and
sound judgement. I was equally impressed with Edward Cullinan and his team and found them very sympathetic in their
dealings with us.

The first crisis came within days of my institution. We were
summoned to the Chancellor of the Diocese, Revd Garth
Moore, who had to adjudicate on the future of the scheme. He
was in charge of one of the City Churches and we had to
appear before him there. Here we encountered a further problem. The Bishop of Southwark had fallen out with his Chancellor. In the end he dropped him and presided himself in the
ecclesiastical Court as he did when he came to Barnes. By now
the Bishop had retired and the new Bishop (Ronnie Bowlby)
had reinstated Garth Moore quite recently. We were the first
case to come before him since being restored to office and as it
turned out to be the scapegoat on whom he could pronounce
his wrath.

We had gathered in the vestry of his Church. This included
a group representing the opposition. As soon as we were
ushered into the Chancellor's presence we realised that this
was not going in our favour. Garth Moore began with a
diatribe against the Bishop of Southwark and then delivered a
judgement which at first sight left us devastated. It did not
seem to leave us much scope for continuing with the scheme.
We felt deflated when we left that morning whereas the
opposition looked rather pleased. However, when we studied
the judgement again in the light of day we found that it left the
door open. It laid down that for every further step in the
rebuilding programme we would have to seek the Chancellor's
permission. This was tedious and frustrating and we now had
to test whether he would stand in our way or let us proceed. In
fact, we found that once he had blown his top he proved quite
fair-minded. As our plans developed we obtained all the permis-
sions we needed.

The next challenge was to raise the money we needed for
the rebuilding. Again, the opposition thought and hoped that

the scheme would fail because we would never raise the funds we needed. Even the Bishop of Kingston sounded a discouraging note when he said to me that if we could raise £100,000 we would be very lucky and that would not be enough to finance the reconstruction. We had nearly £400,000 from the insurance (the Church was underinsured like so many other ecclesiastical buildings) and we reckoned that we would have to find at least another £200,000. That was a tall order. Fortunately, there is a great deal of expertise in a place like Barnes.

We set up an Appeal Committee which was chaired by a banker. We were in good hands with professional advice. We also engaged the services of a fundraiser who introduced us to all the tricks of the trade to embellish our appeal. I learned a great deal during this time about public relations and presentation. It is important that each letter is top copy, not duplicated, that it is topped and tailed individually, that it is sent first class. Otherwise it will just go into the waste paper basket. That meant hard work for some of the scribes who helped us, but it was worthwhile. We went carefully through the book listing all the charities in the United Kingdom and wrote these personalised letters to any charities which might look sympathetically on our appeal. We produced, again with expert help, a brochure setting out the history of the Church and our needs for the restoration.

On 21st April 1982 we formally launched the Appeal in the presence of a number of influential representatives in the local community and beyond. And now the anxious time of waiting began. We had no idea what the response would be and whether the Bishop of Kingston would be proved right. There was still a strong vocal opposition who used the local press and distributed their leaflets throughout Barnes. But there was also a great deal of good will in the community who wanted to see their Church restored.

We held monthly meetings of the Rebuilding Committee, often attended by the architects. They often went on beyond midnight. By the time the Church was completely rebuilt we had held over eighty meetings. The overall structure had been decided before I arrived on the scene, but all the details of interior design and furnishings had still to be settled. Except for the Lady Chapel (which we later named Langton Chapel after Archbishop Stephen Langton) for which some pews were made, I pleaded for chairs for the main body of the Church. There were some initial reservations, but in the end the Committee saw my point. It allowed for greater flexibility. There might be times when we wanted to rearrange the seating, there might be occasions when we wanted to clear the whole floor space (as we did for a youth event). I was also hoping that the Church would be used for concerts or plays and the audience would want to be comfortable. I also suggested a free hanging, simple wooden cross suspended over the altar which did become the focus of the whole building. There were many other details like this to be hammered out. The architects were very patient with us. They listened carefully to our proposals and then came back with sketches for us to approve or reject. Altogether it was a very exciting time to be so closely involved in redesigning a church from scratch.

Although the tower had suffered only minor damage in the fire it was considered wise to take down the bells some of which went back 400 years. They were stored at the Whitechapel Bell Foundry. The first sign that the Church was coming back to life again was in November 1981 when the bells were rehung. On Christmas night the bells rung out over Barnes for the first time since June 1978.

It took nearly another year before the builders moved in. Contrary to the doubts expressed in some quarters the response to the Appeal was quite amazing. In fact, a relatively small part of the total came from charities and commercial firms. Most of it came from the local community. This to me was clear evidence that they wanted their church rebuilt. In the end this evidence silenced the opposition.

In the early summer the architects put the work out to tender. A number of firms had shown interest. It was a good moment, the building trade was looking for work. By the late summer we had raised £140,000, and with the insurance money we had over half a million available. In early September the Chairman of the Rebuilding Committee and I went to the office of Ted Cullinan in North London. When the tenders were opened, six in all, the lowest was within the range of our funds. We were jubilant. It was an ecstatic moment. In a much shorter time than we had dared to hope the reconstruction of the Church was in sight. Messrs Try whose tender we accepted proved a very reliable firm who did a first-class job.

At the end of November, after the Parish Communion in the Hall, about 200 people – congregation, architects, engineers, builders – filed into the ruins of the Church for a brief act of blessing on the work. Next morning the builders moved in. The schedule was completion in fifteen months. The builders kept to it It was exciting to watch the new Church rise from the ashes and for the interior to take shape. Included in the design were vestries and several meeting rooms. The facilities were infinitely better than before. There was the inevitable rush to get the work finished in time and to make the building presentable for the official opening.

On Sunday 26th February 1984, less than six years after the fire, we moved back into St Mary's for the Rehallowing. To the strains of 'Come thou Holy Spirit come' written by Archbishop Stephen Langton we processed in. Ronnie Bowlby, the Bishop of Southwark, led us in an Act of Thanksgiving and Dedication. Carl Davis, the composer who lived almost next to the Church, had written a special anthem. The completed building to which so much prayer and planning had been devoted surpassed my expectations. Thanks to the imaginative design blending old and new we were given a magnificent new place of worship. Since then it has had a number of awards. Architectural students from universities all over the country and from abroad have been to see it. After all, it is not very often that an ancient church is being rebuilt today.

We were still without an organ and the funds did not stretch to include a good instrument. We formed another Committee and launched a separate appeal. We visited a number of Churches where a new organ by well known organ builders had recently been installed and after a great deal of market research chose Peter Collins to build us a new instrument. We managed to raise another £50,000 to add a beautiful new organ a year after the reopening of the Church. Since then we have been blessed with two excellent organists and choirmasters. They have trained a very good choir. The standard of music is very high.

From the moment the Church was open again we had various offers of concerts to help with the fundraising. Quite early on Carl Davis brought a section of the English Chamber Orchestra. It was quite a thrill to have one of the best orchestras playing in the Church. The Barnes Music Society now have regular concerts there and many well known artists have played at St Mary's. I was anxious to encourage the use of the Church for music partly because I love music though sadly I don't play an instrument, partly because a Church building seems the right setting for heavenly music. But I was also anxious to encourage people in the community who do not necessarily go to Church to come and feel at home there while they enjoy good music in that setting. In our secular culture anything that will draw people across the threshold into the House of God is at least one step for them. Sadly, for many people the Church is a place that they would still like to see in the centre of the community even though they stay away from it. How can we encourage them to come and feel at home in it? Again, right from the start we formed the Friends of St Mary's, a group of members of the congregation who would man the Church each morning to guard it and to welcome visitors. At least for part of the day the Church is open for people to drop in just to look or be quiet or to pray.

The rebuilding of the Church and the appeal to raise the necessary funds took a considerable amount of my time. But it did not detract from the other equally important task, i.e. the building up of the congregation. I spent every spare minute visiting as many people as possible – members of the Church, former members who had gone away and people in the community whom I wanted to meet. The result was that gradually the Church grew in numbers. I know that numbers is not everything, but the steady increase was a sign that people recognized that the Church was once again on the map. Barnes is full of good and able people. It was heartening to see that more and more of them began to make their contribution to the life of the Church. For our first Christmas and thereafter first the Hall and then the Church (with twice the seating capacity) was full to overflowing three times over (midnight, Parish Communion and Family Service). Once the new building was open my dream of having a dynamic Church at the centre of the community came true.

To make this possible I was supported by a very good team.

I have already mentioned Viera Gray, first as deaconess and then made deacon. She was widely regarded in the parish as the 'saint' and so she was. Her spiritual influence not only among Church people, but in the wider community as well was enormous. Many people went to her for counselling. Her physical energy was boundless. She was constantly flitting round the parish on her bicycle. And yet there was nothing restless or hurried about her (as there might have been about me), she radiated the serenity of Christ. In my address at the Memorial Service in Southwark Cathedral after her untimely and tragic death in a road accident I ended with this quotation about Jesus 'Someone who did not separate religion and life into neat little compartments, but lived his life to the full, passionately committed to the life and growth of everyone he met. He spent himself constantly in going out to people and meeting them in their need accepting and loving them completely'. That sounded very much like Viera, too.

We also had Raymond Chapman, Professor at LSE and a non-stipendiary priest who lived in the parish and assisted most faithfully throughout the time I was there. For a time we even had Richard Harries living in the parish when he was Dean of King's. He was busy most weekends, but helped out from time to time until he moved to Oxford when he became Bishop. During the nine years I was served by outstanding and loyal Churchwardens. Soon after I came to Barnes I was told of somebody who had been a leading light in the congregation, but had become disillusioned like so many others and had dropped out. I visited him and immediately recognised in him a potential future warden. When the time came to find a new Warden I invited him. He accepted and proved a great support during the difficult and demanding years of the rebuilding of the Church and beyond.

We had very good relations with the other Churches in Barnes. Since working in a united College in Nigeria I had always felt particularly close to the Methodists and this was also the case in Barnes. I always took part in their moving Covenant Service at the beginning of the New Year. There was a Council of Churches in which I played an active part. Each year there were a number of ecumenical events and eventually we entered into an ecumenical Covenant which included the

Baptists and Roman Catholics as well. We also had a Mission in Barnes which was led by the Franciscans and in which again all the Churches took part.

We had three Anglican Churches in Barnes. The Churchmanship of the other two was higher than ours, but that added to the richness of the Anglican tradition. As Barnes was such an integrated community I felt from early days that it was a nonsense and detrimental to the Christian Mission that the three Churches should each go their own way. Barnes seemed an obvious place for a Team Ministry where each Church would still have its own distinctive style of worship and identity, but where the clergy worked as a team and the congregations were closely related to each other. Initially there was not much enthusiasm for such an idea, but as time went on the relations between the three churches improved considerably. The clergy met weekly. An excellent joint magazine *Barnes in Common* was published. The joint Mission in 1988 again helped to bring us together. Towards the end of my time with the encouragement of the diocese we pressed the case for moving into a properly constituted Team Ministry. But such changes cannot be hurried. Congregations are jealous of their rights and afraid of what they might have to give up. My successor was appointed as Team Rector Designate and I hope that before long the three Anglican Churches will be seen as one within the wider community.

I think it is worth trying out various experiments in the attempt to enlarge the scope of the Gospel. Some fail, but other succeed. For a time we ran Supper Evenings. One couple would invite a number of other couples for a meal. To these evenings we would also invite a good Christian speaker who would introduce a discussion after supper. Again for a time I led a Book Group. It was quite high-powered and a good cross section of professional people. We would choose a book, read a chapter at a time and then discuss it.

Arising out of the Mission we started a Men's Breakfast Group which used to meet monthly early on a Saturday morning. This was the most convenient time to bring men together. After a substantial breakfast a member of the Group would raise a subject and then throw it open for discussion. Among our study groups I was anxious to introduce one specifically for business people as many of them wrestle daily with difficult ethical problems in their work in the city. We brought in experts to help us with the consideration of these issues.

One of the most ambitious projects we embarked on was a Marriage Preparation Scheme. This was different from the one that Jean and I had run in Putney. This time we recruited a number of younger Christian couples in the three Churches. The Vicar of Heston brought over some of his couples who in turn had been trained by a Catholic group. The training was extremely rigorous and personally quite demanding. By the end of it, after almost a year, we had a first class team. Each couple would meet with the pair who were shortly to be married in one of our Churches. There was a co-ordinator who ran the scheme and would match our team with these couples. From time to time the team would meet to review their work. Their keen commitment to this important work has been quite remarkable. This kind of preparation does not prevent the alarming rate of marriage breakdowns, but one hopes that it makes these couples more aware of each other's needs and more prepared to work at their relationships.

While I was in Barnes I was asked to help with one or two matters in the diocese. Although I was full stretched in the parish I welcomed these opportunities to help in the wider sphere of the Church. Otherwise there is a danger that one might become too parochially minded. There was quite a long interregnum in the leadership of the Lay Training Team of the diocese. I was asked to keep an eye on them during that time and to chair their weekly Team meetings. I was and still am very committed to the training and development of men and women in the lay ministry of the Church. The diocese had a splendid team and I enjoyed sharing with them in their efforts to train the laity in the diocese.

Soon after I came to Southwark the Bishop appointed me as one of his Examining Chaplains. This meant among other things that initially I had to see men, and later women as well, who felt a call to the ordained ministry. I had to make recommendations to the Director of Ordinands. Later I became a Bishop's Selector which meant going to some of the Selection Conferences run by ACCM (now ABM). This I found one of the most demanding, but also most worthwhile responsibilities that I have been involved in during my ministry. The candidates come for a 48 hours' residential conference at one of a number of places throughout England. For them and for the selectors they are two very concentrated days filled with interviews, written and group exercises and worship. The selector has to do his or her homework beforehand to be well prepared. There is hardly a spare moment for the Staff during the conference. And once the candidates have departed the real work of the selectors begins to consider each candidate and to arrive at a decision. Sometimes when it is a borderline case they agonise until they come to a common mind. It think it is a fair process.

The prior reports and recommendations (although some of these are not worth the paper they are written on), the interviews and the exercises give a fairly comprehensive impression of the candidate. What I have found so deeply moving at these Conferences is to meet a cross section of women and men from all walks of life and all ages who have a strong conviction that they have a vocation to the sacred ministry. Sometimes they hold lucrative and responsible jobs in the secular world and are prepared to give it up for a relatively poorly paid priesthood. To me it is a sure sign that despite the drop in numbers the Church is not spiritually in decline, but that there are all the time these indications of new life.

When I came to Barnes in 1981 I knew that this was probably going to be my last post. I was very reluctant to leave the parish. It was such a constant joy to worship and to lead the worship in such a beautiful Church. There were now many flourishing activities, and a lively and responsive congregation. St Mary's, Barnes, had truly experienced a resurrection, both material and spiritual. We had made many wonderful friends both inside and outside the Church and we enjoyed living in such a lively and caring community. I was anxious to leave while the Church was going well and before it was becoming too much for me. It now needed a younger man to carry it forward and hopefully to bring the Team Ministry into being. I, therefore, decided to resign in the summer of 1990 shortly before my sixty-sixth birthday. We had the usual presentations and farewells. On Sunday 10th June I celebrated for the last time the Parish Communion and after a big reception in the Church Hall walked back to the Rectory. I suddenly realised that after nearly thirty-eight years my active ministry had come to an end. Three weeks later we moved to our Cottage in Hampshire which we had acquired four years earlier in preparation for our retirement.

# 15

# Reflections

As I look back over my life and especially over the more than forty years in the ordained ministry I can only say that I have been indeed a most fortunate man. God has been so good to me in so many ways. Even the years of adversity under Hitler and especially the traumatic experiences of forced labour turned out to be a blessing. They have given me a more profound understanding of suffering and adversity and of the power of Christ to heal and redeem.

I have been particularly fortunate in sharing my life with Jean. It is never easy to be a clergy wife. With all the demands that other people make upon a priest's time and attention wife and family often take second place. I am very conscious that I am no exception in this respect and that I have not given enough time and attention to my home and family. After bringing up the family Jean trained as a Health Visitor and became a very competent and highly regarded carer in that profession. She retired shortly before I did. While she was working – in Kingston, Richmond and Sheen – we were both fully stretched. Both of us were fulfilled in our respective callings.

We have been richly blessed with our three children. All three are married and we are very happy with the partners they have chosen We seem to have started something with our spell in Nigeria and our love for Africa. At least two of our children have continued this link. Ruth first went with CMS to the Southern Sudan and then after her marriage to Ian they worked for Tearfund in Guinea-Bissau. Hilary married Giles whose home is in Zimbabwe and they are working at present in Khartoum. To date we have been blessed with four lovely grandchildren.

My mother died in 1986. My father taught himself Braille when he was in his nineties. He gave up preaching when he was about 98. He was mentally alert right to the end and died at the age of 101. They made a new life for themselves for the second half of their lifespan in Fulham, Dalston, Hampstead and Stanmore and had a host of friends.

We had seven very rewarding years in Nigeria. We are so glad that we had the opportunity to work on the African continent. I think we have the advantage of evaluating news from there better because we have actually lived there. We can understand some of their problems because we have seen them at close quarters. It has been said that when you have been to Africa you leave part of your heart behind. I think that would be true of us.

Until recently I chaired a support group for the Nigerian Chaplaincy in the UK, based in London. This was mainly for the care of Nigerian students in this country and was headed up successively by two first-class Nigerian Anglican priests. It involved me in a visit to Nigeria in October 1986, well over twenty years after we had left. I saw great changes since that time. I was struck with the population explosion in Lagos and Ibadan and even more with the expansion of the Church everywhere. Fortunately I also managed at long last to visit the new Immanuel College near the University of Ibadan.

It was also my good fortune that I was called to serve in the two parishes of St Margaret, Putney and St Mary, Barnes. Altogether we had twenty-one years in that part of London and they were very fruitful and rewarding years. I am particularly glad that I was offered the challenge of being involved in the rebuilding of the Church and congregation in Barnes. Those nine years were really the culmination of my ministry. Although I come from the evangelical tradition and shall always be grateful for its emphasis on the Gospel and evangelism and personal faith I never regarded myself as a rigid 'conservative'. I owe much to people like Max Warren with a more liberal approach and a wider perspective. In the course of my ministry I began to value also the more Catholic tradition within the Anglican Church with its emphasis on the Sacraments and the beauty of holiness. I feel at home in all traditions now and can worship happily anywhere, be it Anglican, Nonconformist or Roman Catholic, provided it is sincere and meaningful. When we are in France on holiday we love to go to the local Catholic Church with its simplicity and participation of the laity. In fact, I do not really want to have any party labels attached to my Christian faith. I am sure that when we go to heaven we shall not be asked whether we have been conservatives, liberals, radicals, evangelicals or Anglo-Catholics, but simply whether we have loved and served our Lord. I simply want to be a Christian, with all my faults following him whose name I bear hopefully right to the end.

Throughout my ministry there have been several major concerns. First, for the Gospel and its proclamation. The Christian Mission at home and abroad has always been vital to me. It took us to Nigeria to help with the building up of the ministry there. I have always maintained a great interest in the missionary work of the Church. The Church Missionary Society has played an important role in my life and I was profoundly influenced by the thinking and writings of Max Warren and John V. Taylor. I have taken part in a number of evangelistic missions and sought to lead people to faith in Jesus Christ. I have a great respect for Dr Billy Graham and the impact he has made worldwide through his crusades. I am deeply puzzled how one does evangelise in a predominantly secular society where the gulf between those inside and outside the church is now considerable. While I am writing this we have now been for several years into the Decade of Evangelism and my impression is that we are not making much headway. We do not seem to be able to communicate effectively the Good News to those who consider it meaningless or irrelevant. We lack the confidence to declare the faith outside the Church. We are nervous and embarrassed to nail our colours to the mast. I ask myself why that is so. There is a climate of indifference in the West which is almost worse than active opposition. And we are somehow drawn into its spiral. I was recently taken to task by Bishop Lesslie Newbigin, and rightly so. At a meeting I asked him whether in view of the present decline of the Church he could make any prophetic comment on the future of Christianity. He replied 'what kind of question is this? Surely if we believe in the risen Christ the future of the Christian Church is never in doubt'. Indeed! We need to be reminded that God is the Lord of the Church and that he will look after it. 'The gates of hell shall not prevail against it.' Alongside some of the discouragements there are also plenty of signs here and there where the Spirit is at work and where there is new life.

My second concern has been about the unity of the Church. As I mentioned above, in the Sixties, especially after the Nottingham Conference, there seemed to be every indication that we were on the way to a united Church. In the early Seventies came the sad setback of the Anglican/Methodist reunion. And since then the movement towards organic unity has lost more and more of its momentum. However, there are plenty of ecumenical experiments and projects on the local level all over the country. It almost looks as though institutional unity between denominations is not meant to be for the time being. I have never quite understood why the Eucharist which is surely the symbol of unity becomes a stumbling block in some quarters. One of the most moving experiences I can remember was when I have broken bread with members of other churches and we have shared in that spiritual and sacramental unity. Sadly, so often we put man made, legalistic obstacles in the way and make the whole process of unity so complicated.

Having said that it is also true that on the pastoral and local level relationships between the Churches, especially with the Roman Catholics, are much better today and for that we must be thankful. We certainly do not want *any* kind of uniformity. We need the Quakers (or Society of Friends) on the one side and the Roman Catholics on the other and every shade in between. However, I am quite sure that in the life to come there will not be any of these labels and divisions. We shall all be gathered round the throne of God and simply worship and adore him.

I have to confess that I am a bookworm and that I have always had a love for theological books and study. I owe a great deal to many writers and thinkers. If I wanted to single out any from the large number of authors I would mention Stephen Neill and Lesslie Newbigin, and again John V. Taylor. All three writers have one thing in common – the Mission of the Church. For the last fifteen years or more I have been fortunate to belong to a Reading Party. It was started by John Lovell, a Vicar in Southwark Diocese. Each year it brought together a group of clergy, some with a CMS background. Some of us had links with St Julians and after the first two years we were allowed to hold our Reading Parties at this beautiful and congenial place. John Lovell died tragically of a heart attack and I took over to organise our annual get-together. We choose a book and part of the time read it and the other part we discuss it. We are grateful to St Julians who continue to offer us their hospitality. These opportunities to study together are very stimulating. The membership has changed a little over the years, but the core of members is still the same which I suppose means that it is appreciated.

My love of preaching I owe in the first place to Dr (now Lord) Coggan. He used to take us in Homiletics when I was at the London College of Divinity and gave us a real grounding in the proclamation of the Word. I always remember the importance he placed on the 'indicative' and the 'imperative'. The indicative (as he explains in his book *The Sacrament of the Word*) is to declare what God has done, is doing and will do. The imperative is to go on to teach Christian ethics. As he says 'you cannot preach the indicatives without going on to expound and apply their implications'. I was particularly fortunate to catch a love of preaching from a great preacher. I wonder whether that same emphasis on preaching is found in our theological Colleges today. Sadly, preaching has been largely reduced to a ten minute slot in the Parish Communion. It is difficult in so short a space to expound God's Word adequately. But that lays upon the preacher an even greater discipline to condense the eternal message in such a way that it still comes across to the person in the pew.

I am glad that I have seen in my lifetime the ordination of women to the priesthood in the Church of England. I had the privilege of taking part in one of these ordinations at Southwark Cathedral. I am fully aware of the arguments for and against women priests. They have been rehearsed over and over again for the past ten years and more. But I still fail to understand the objections, especially when Synod voted years ago that there were no fundamental theological objections. In every other profession women now play increasingly an equal role with men. Both man and woman are made in the image of God and women have been endowed just the same with spiritual graces. To argue that Jesus' disciples and then apostles were men does not convince me. Of course, Jesus would have chosen men in his time. Women were considered inferior 2,000 years ago. They are not today. This kind of argument takes no account of the Holy Spirit 'who leads us into all truth'. Many things have changed in the Church over the centuries. I believe that in our time the Holy Spirit convicts us that women should be given a full and equal share in the ordained ministry. If I needed any convincing it was during the time that I was working with Viera Gray, our deacon in Barnes. Admittedly, she was an exceptional person. But like so many other women she brought into the Church gifts of insight and gentleness and empathy which we men do not seem to possess in the same measure. Her ministry was in many ways more effective than mine. I am confident that from now on when women can play their full part in the priestly ministry the Church will be the richer for it.

There have been disappointments and setbacks and frustrations in the course of my ministry. There are regrets that I have missed opportunities, there were situations which I would handle differently if I was faced with them today. There were hard and painful lessons which I had to learn. But I think I am completely honest when I say that I have never had any regrets about embarking on the sacred ministry of the Church. I thank God that through the war time experiences he led me to faith in him and then led me on to serve him in the full time work of the Church. I am glad that I was engaged in it during the last forty years. I have found them an exciting period in the history of the Church. They have been a testing time and have seen many radical changes. On the whole, I think, they have been positive and have made the Church perhaps leaner, but stronger. The challenge is now, as in all ages, to proclaim the Good News 'in season and out of season' and to stress in this secular and materialistic age the vital need of moral and spiritual values in our society and our individual lives. I am confident that the Holy Spirit is alive and active in his Church and that there are signs of spiritual renewal in many places which do not hit the headlines.

When I first started reading the Bible, before I was a Christian, I turned to the Psalms. They are a treasure house and I still derive much comfort and inspiration from them. In Psalm 84 the Psalmist says 'Blessed is the man whose strength is in thee: in whose heart are thy ways. Who going through the vale of misery use it for a well . . .' I suppose that last phrase is a good summary of my life. The vale of misery turned most wonderfully into a well, the well of God's goodness and grace. From this well I have drawn over and over again. I trust that it will sustain and strengthen me for many years to come.

# Index